ISAIAH BERLIN

ISAIAH BERLIN

John Gray

PRINCETON UNIVERSITY PRESS

PRINCETON, NEW JERSEY

First published in Great Britain by HarperCollins*Publishers*, 1995

Library of Congress Cataloging-in-Publication Data
Gray, John, 1948–
Isaiah Berlin / John Gray.
p.   cm.
Includes bibliographical references and index.
ISBN 0-691-02635-1 (alk. paper)
1. Berlin, Isaiah, Sir—Contributions in political science.
2. Berlin, Isaiah, Sir—Contributions in philosophy.   I. Title.
JC257.B47G73   1996
320'.01—dc20   95-42249

This book has been composed in Trump Medieval

Princeton University Press books are printed on acid-free paper
and meet the guidelines for permanence and durability of the
Committee on Production Guidelines for Book Longevity
of the Council on Library Resources

Printed in the United States of America
by Princeton Academic Press

10 9 8 7 6 5 4 3 2 1

Contents

Acknowledgements

There are many people and institutions without whose support and assistance this book could not have been written. The Principal and Fellows of my College have given me periods of leave from my duties there without which my thoughts on the issues raised by the thought of Isaiah Berlin would never have germinated. My debt to my College is profound. The book itself was written during two periods of residence at the Social Philosophy and Policy Center at Bowling Green State University in Ohio. I am indebted to the Directors and staff of the Center for their manifold help in enabling me to complete this project.

I owe a special debt of gratitude to Dr Henry Hardy, Fellow of Wolfson College, Oxford, Isaiah Berlin's editor and one of his literary executors. The generosity and goodwill, along with the patience and erudition, which Henry Hardy has shown me throughout this venture have gone far beyond any imaginable call of duty on his part. I am sure that the book could not have been completed in anything like its present form without his unfailing support.

Without the initial stimulus of a telephone call from my publisher, Stuart Proffitt of HarperCollins, I would not have dreamt of trying my hand at this book. For his confidence in the project, and his comments on it, I am very grateful.

A number of people have given me written and oral comments on the book. I wish especially to thank David Conway, Henry Hardy and G. W. Smith for their detailed written comments on early drafts. Discussions with Roger Hausheer and Loren Lomasky have clarified my thoughts on many of the issues it addresses. Conversations over many years with Joseph Raz have left a deep mark on my thought of which there are many traces in the book.

To express my debt to Isaiah Berlin himself is a task beyond my powers. For over twenty years my thoughts have grown under the stimulus of his extraordinary conversation. My enormous intellectual debts to him will be obvious to any reader of this book or of my other writings. At the same time, he has not seen this study, and neither the interpretation of his thought, nor the critical assessment of it that I attempt, has his authority. I could not have written it as I have done if I did not know Isaiah Berlin as I do, but it is my book, not his, all the same. All the usual disclaimers, which apply to all those who helped me with this book, apply with special force to Berlin himself.

John Gray
Jesus College, Oxford
July 1994

Introduction

If writing a study of the thought of Isaiah Berlin is a daunting task, the explanation is not to be found in any obscurity in his writings, which are marvellously clear. Nor, though they cover a vast range of subjects and writers, are his works so disparate as to lack common themes. If anything, the opposite is the case. The central claim of this book is that all of Berlin's work is animated by a single idea of enormous subversive force. This is the idea, which I call value-pluralism, that ultimate human values are objective but irreducibly diverse, that they are conflicting and often uncombinable, and that sometimes when they come into conflict with one another they are incommensurable; that is, they are not comparable by any rational measure. Elucidating and assessing this idea will occupy much of this book. Its implication for political philosophy is that the idea of a perfect society in which all genuine ideals and goods are achieved is not merely utopian; it is incoherent. Political life, like moral life, abounds in radical choices between rival goods and evils, where reason leaves us in the lurch and whatever is done involves loss and sometimes tragedy. I call the political outlook which this idea inspires in Berlin's work *agonistic liberalism*, taking the expression from the Greek word *agon*, whose meaning covers both competition or rivalry and the conflicts of characters in tragic drama. By contrast with the dominant liberalisms of our time, which in their claim that fundamental liberties, rights or claims of justice are (or indeed must be) compatible and harmonious are Panglossian in their optimism, Berlin's is a stoical and tragic liberalism of unavoidable conflict and irreparable loss among inherently rivalrous values. Because it does not share the hopes (or illusions) of the dominant liberalisms, of our own day and in the past, about the compatibility of basic liberties and equalities, or subscribe to the Whiggish philosophies of history with which these liberalisms are associated and upon which they depend, Berlin's political thought offers the liberal intellectual tradition a new lease on life. This is so, even if, as I shall argue, there may be an unresolved conflict in Berlin's thought between his doctrine of value-pluralism and the historicist conception of human nature to which he holds on the one hand and the universalist claims of any species of traditional liberalism on the other. It is in resolving this conflict in Berlin's thought, which may be interpreted as a tension between its debts to Vico and Herder on the one hand and its affinities with the liberalism of John Stuart Mill on the other, by developing its historicist claims and reconceiving liberalism as a particular form of life, with no universal claim on reason, foundation in human nature or privileged place in history, that I take a step for which there is no clear authority in Berlin's writings, and which he might well be reluctant to follow. On this Vichian and Herderian interpretation of Berlin, the bottom line in his thought is not a liberal *agon* but agonistic pluralism.

The profound originality and subversive quality of Berlin's thought help to explain an otherwise anomalous fact – the absence, until very recently, of any book-length study of it.[1] It is true, also, that the very scope of Berlin's intellectual activity is daunting. In this study I have had to make several strategic omissions, each defensible, but each of them regrettable in that it involves leaving out an important dimension of the man or his work. I have not made use of the large corpus of unpublished writings on many themes in the possession of Henry Hardy, but have confined myself entirely to published sources. I have said little of Berlin's early philosophical papers on topics in the theory of knowledge and of meaning, aside from noting in them a sustained argument against the positivist reduction of all meaningful discourse to a single mode that is analogous with, and perhaps anticipates, his later attack on monism in the theory of value. I have not addressed Berlin's many important contributions to Russian studies, save indirectly or in passing; nor his work as a wartime political observer (of which some elements are available in published form as *Washington Despatches*); or his profound knowledge and love of music. I have not attempted to describe his many friendships, which must await the publication of the biography being written of him by Michael Ignatieff. Nor have I attempted to illuminate the links between Berlin's personality and conversation, which are extraordinary in their powers of imaginative empathy, and his thought, which constantly affirms the reality, validity and human intelligibility of values and forms of life very different from our own. Instead I have focused on his political thought, and on the moral theory, and the conception of philosophy, that it expresses and embodies, since it seems to me that this captures best Berlin's most enduring intellectual achievement, and the permanent mark he has made upon liberal thought.

I outline Berlin's life only in so far as it seems relevant to his thought. Born in Riga on 6 June 1909, Sir Isaiah Berlin, O.M., is descended, like Yehudi Menuhin, from the Chabad Hasidim, now commonly known as Lubavich. His grandparents, but not his parents, were pious Hasidim. He was brought up in Riga speaking Russian and German. His family moved from Riga to Andreapol in 1915, and on to Petrograd in 1917, where he witnessed the first Russian Revolution in February 1917 and the Bolshevik coup of November, then moved to England in 1921 after a brief spell back in Latvia. His grandfathers, an uncle, an aunt, and three cousins were murdered by the Nazis in Riga in 1941. His schooling was at St Paul's and his university education at Corpus Christi College, Oxford. Except for a period of three years, when he lived first in New York, then in Washington, working for the British government, and a brief period in Moscow in 1945, Berlin has spent his life in Oxford, where he remains a Fellow of All Souls College, having also held the Chichele Chair in Social and Political Theory there (1957–67). He was the first President of Wolfson College (1966–75) and was President of the British Academy from 1974–8. He continues to live most of the time in Oxford, talking, writing and publishing.

Isaiah Berlin is often compared to David Hume. The comparison is perhaps not altogether misleading, but it leaves out much that is essential in the man. Like Hume, Berlin gave up philosophy to practise history – though, as with Hume's history of England, Berlin's studies in intellectual history are exemplars of his philosophical outlook. If he shares with Hume a profound intellectual gaiety, a love of clarity in thought and writing and a relish for the ironies of history, Berlin has in him other passions, altogether absent from the genial Hume. These passions come from the elements of his plural inheritance that are not English but Russian and Jewish;[2] they are his passion for ideas and his sense of the tragic in human life. Berlin has said, with much truth, that he was formed, intellectually, by Anglo-American philosophy and by Kant;[3] and of the profundity of his understanding of, and absorption in, British empiricism in particular there can be no doubt. Yet there is a deep difference between the sometimes desiccated discourse of professional Anglo-American philosophy and Berlin's writings, which springs, perhaps, not only from Berlin's inimitable style and almost clairvoyant powers of imaginative empathy for thinkers utterly different from himself, but from a conception of intellectual life, and of the responsibility of the intellectual, that is not English but Russian. Berlin's lifework, though it embodies the standards of rigour and clarity that distinguish British empiricism at its best, exemplifies a conception of the role of the intellectual that is not well-recognized in Britain – as one who communicates a conception of human life as a whole – and the roots of which are in Berlin's case Russian. The conception of human life that animates Berlin's work – which Noel Annan has called 'the truest and the most moving of all interpretations of life that my own generation made'[4] – is a tragic one, resistant to the claims of any theodicy, whose sources are, I believe, in aspects of Berlin's Jewish heritage. It is the intermingling in his plural inheritance of these diverse elements that makes Berlin's thought a delicate skein of subtle ideas which it is the aim of this modest study to unravel.

1 The Idea of Freedom

What Montesquieu means by liberty is not to be found in his formal – and commonplace – definition of this concept as consisting in the right to do what the laws do not forbid, but in his exposition of other social and political ideas which throw light on his general scale of values. Montesquieu is, above all, not a thinker obsessed by some single principle, seeking to order and explain everything in terms of some central moral or metaphysical category in terms of which all truths must be formulated. He is not a monist but a pluralist, his virtuosity reaches its highest peak, he is most himself, when he tries to convey a culture or an outlook or a system of values different from his own and from that of the majority of his readers.

Isaiah Berlin, 'Montesquieu'[1]

The idea of freedom that animates all of Berlin's work, like his system of ideas as a whole, is at once much more original, and far more subversive of received intellectual tradition in philosophy, than is commonly perceived. It is a commonplace that Berlin cautions against 'positive' conceptions of freedom which view it in terms of rational self-determination, or autonomy, and that he does so in favour of a 'negative' account of freedom in which it is conceived as the absence of constraints imposed by others. Less well understood are Berlin's reasons for preferring a negative conception of freedom. Few would accuse Berlin of denying that freedom may legitimately be conceived in terms of autonomy, since his acknowledgements that there have in the history of thought been such conceptions are too frequent, and too unequivocal, to be ignored; but his grounds for thinking that positive views of freedom are inherently flawed, and so perennially liable to abuse, are little understood. Again, it is a truism of intellectual history that Berlin rejects determinism in the human world, and, in particular, the applications of it that have issued in doctrines of historical inevitability. And it is widely understood, though less clearly, that the cornerstone of his thought is his rejection of monism in ethics – his insistence that fundamental human values are many, that they are often in conflict and rarely, if ever, *necessarily* harmonious, and that some at least of these conflicts are among incommensurables – conflicts among values for which there is no single, common standard of measurement or arbitration. These elements in Berlin's thought are recognizable, and intelligible, readily enough, to most recent philosophers and moral and political theorists in the Anglo-American world.

It is the argument of this book, however, that these ideas of Berlin's, rightly interpreted and understood, cohere to form a conception of human life whose subversive originality is as yet very poorly apprehended, and whose applications in political philosophy – in yielding what I term an agonistic liberalism, a liberalism of conflict and unavoidable loss among rivalrous goods and evils – are hardly appreciated at all. If I am right that Berlin's work contains ideas of great profundity and subversive power, one may reasonably ask why this is not widely acknowledged in the world of professional philosophy, where the impact of his thought, though far from negligible, has hardly been decisive. In part, no doubt, the explanation is to be found in Berlin's professed abandonment, after the Second World War, of first-order philosophical work, in favour of intellectual history. But this can hardly be the whole explanation. It is true that much of Berlin's work, indeed the greater part of it, has been in the form of essays in the history of ideas, in which the thought of celebrated as well as obscure theorists is subject to imaginative reconstruction and analytical dissection. We think at once of his essays on Vico, Herder, Hamann, Mill, Maistre, Herzen, and many others. Yet not all of Berlin's *oeuvre* has been in this mode; his famous lecture on liberty was a straightforward exercise in political philosophy, supported by many illuminating historical references and analogies, but standing on its own feet as a piece of philosophical reasoning.

The deeper explanation for the slight impact of Berlin's work on the mainstream tradition in philosophy in our time lies elsewhere – in its divergence from, and undermining of, the forms of rationalism that have dominated moral and political thought in the English-speaking world over the past century. By rationalism is here meant the view that philosophical inquiry can not merely illuminate, but also provide solutions for, the dilemmas we confront in moral and political practice. This rationalist view Berlin has always resolutely rejected. His reasons for rejecting it have little, if anything, in common with the critique of moral and political rationalism offered us by contemporary conservative philosophers such as Michael Oakeshott. Berlin rejects the view, found in Oakeshott,[2] that dilemmas insoluble by reason can be resolved by a return to tradition, so long as it has not been 'scribbled on' by rationalist philosophers, since he believes – surely correctly – that the idea of an uncorrupted text of common life, whether in Oakeshott or Maistre, is a mere illusion: we have no reason to suppose that practice or tradition is coherent. For Berlin, philosophy may illuminate the incoherences of practice, but it cannot resolve them. More radically yet, Berlin's work embodies a challenge to the foundational tenets of the Western intellectual tradition itself, the upshot of which is to limit the scope and authority of philosophy as an intellectual discipline. The implication of Berlin's thought for philosophical method is that the conception of the prescriptive authority of philosophy, and its pretensions to govern practice, which pervades the work of Aristotle, of Plato, of Hobbes, of Spinoza, of Kant, of J. S. Mill and (in a distinct but no less manifest way) of at least the earlier Rawls, say, cannot be accepted: philosophy's pretensions must be far humbler.

Philosophy remains for Berlin vitally important: he tells us that 'The goal of philosophy is always the same, to assist men to understand themselves and thus operate in the open, and not wildly, in the dark.'[3] Nevertheless, the hopes that inspire the philosopher cannot encompass, if Berlin is right, the prospect of a theory or a set of principles that will resolve the dilemmas of practical life, political or moral, since it is one of Berlin's principal contentions that some of these dilemmas are *au fond* insoluble, radical and tragic, and undecidable by rational reflection. Philosophy can hope to illuminate these dilemmas and to straighten out crookednesses in our thought about them; it cannot hope to do more than that. Berlin's thought demands a revision of the received conception of philosophy itself, as this has been exemplified throughout most of the Western tradition.

The species of liberalism which Berlin's work embodies is a deeply distinctive and decidedly original one that is at odds both with the schools of liberal thought recently dominant in the Anglo-American world and with the older traditions of liberalism from which these newer developments spring. As it is expressed in the work of Rawls and Dworkin, Hayek, Nozick, and Gauthier, all of recent liberalism turns on a conception of rational choice, whether Kantian or Millian, Lockean or Hobbesian in content, from which liberal principles are supposedly derived. If, in J. S. Mill, liberal principles are adopted as rational strategies for the maximal promotion of general well-being – as devices for the maximization of utility – then in John Rawls, late as much as early, they are adopted as rational terms of co-operation among persons having no comprehensive conception of the good in common. In Berlin's *agonistic liberalism*, by contrast, the value of freedom derives from the limits of rational choice. Berlin's agonistic liberalism – his liberalism of conflict among inherently rivalrous goods – grounds itself on the radical choices we must make among incommensurables, not upon rational choice. Further, it denies that the structure of liberties appropriate to a liberal society can be derived from any theory, or stated in any system of principles, since the choice among conflicting liberties is often a choice among incommensurables. In this respect, if I am not mistaken, Berlin's agonistic liberalism delivers a fatal blow to the varieties of liberal utilitarianism, of theories of fundamental rights and of contractarian theorizing, that are the stock in trade of recent liberal political philosophy, and which have a genuine pedigree in earlier traditions of liberal thought. His is an unfamiliar and challenging liberalism that is subversive of the rationalist foundations of all the traditional varieties of liberal thought. The only comparable liberalism in recent political philosophy, one to which we shall have occasion to refer repeatedly, is found in the work of Joseph Raz,[4] which may be fruitfully compared with that of Berlin. It is the radical criticisms it contains of conceptions of rational choice, and of their uses as foundations of liberalism, that most deeply accounts for the comparatively shallow influence of Berlin's thought on recent moral and political philosophy, which persists in being animated by a species of rationalism that Berlin's work undermines.

It is not, to be sure, that Berlin is an irrationalist, an enemy of Enlightenment, for, like one of his patron saints, David Hume, he remains committed to a central element of the Enlightenment project, namely the illumination of the human world by rational inquiry. It is nonetheless the case that Berlin's rejection of the species of rationalism for which the dilemmas of practice are in the end illusory, that rationalism which goes back to Plato and perhaps to Socrates, and which animates many of the central thinkers of the Enlightenment, expresses a conception of human nature which is hard to square with that of the Enlightenment. It is a view of man as inherently unfinished and incomplete, as essentially self-transforming and only partly determinate, of man as at least partly the author of himself and not subject comprehensively to any natural order. It is also a view of man in which the idea of a common or constant human nature has little place, one in which the capacity of man as

a supremely inventive species to fashion for itself a plurality
of divergent natures is central. Berlin's rejection of the view
of man as a natural object in a natural order, subject to
natural laws and intelligible in his behaviour and nature by
reference to those laws, and his pluralist conception of man
as a self-transforming species which invents a variety of
natures for itself, puts him closer to the Romantics and to
the thinkers of what he calls the Counter-Enlightenment
than it does to the Enlightenment, whose values of intellectual emancipation and rational self-criticism he nevertheless steadfastly defends.

The conception of human nature to which I have referred,
and which recurs throughout Berlin's work, presupposes a
rejection of determinism as that view applies to human conduct. The aspiration of a science of human behaviour, which
is 'nomological' or law-governed in structure in that it generates explanations and predictions of human events by reference to laws of the sort we find in the natural sciences, and
which was a central project of the European Enlightenment
in the work of such figures as Helvétius, Holbach, Diderot,
and even (despite his attack on induction) David Hume, is
rejected by Berlin. It must not be supposed that he advances,
or seeks to advance, a demonstrative refutation of human
determinism. His argument is instead against compatibilism – the philosophical theory that nothing of substance
in our ordinary moral and political thought, discourse and
practice need be affected by the truth of determinism. Berlin
has always argued against this view – the dominant view
in English-speaking empiricist philosophy. For Berlin, such
practices as praise and blame, such sentiments as resentment and gratitude, presuppose that the agents who are their
objects could have done otherwise than they did when they
evoked our responses. He accordingly rejects the justification of punishment, advanced by utilitarians in this compa-
tibilist tradition, as a sort of technology of deterrence:
whatever it may be, it cannot be *only* that, since it incorporates judgements of deservingness and culpability which

again presuppose that agents can act otherwise than they do, all conditions prior to the act in question remaining the same. Nor does Berlin accept the commonest empiricist version of compatibilism, which J. S. Mill espoused – the doctrine of self-determinism, which says that we are free in so far as we can deliberately alter our characters and dispositions if we so wish. For, as Berlin points out,[5] if determinism is true, if we are links in a universal chain of natural causation, then our very desire to amend our character is itself causally necessitated: it could not be otherwise than it is, nor more efficacious than it proves to be. This doctrine of self-determinism, with which Mill in the *System of Logic*[6] sought to dispel the nightmare of determinism, is an illusion: determinism *remains* a nightmare.

It remains a nightmare because its truth would entail the abandonment of a vast complex of practices and sentiments that form essential elements of our ordinary conception of ourselves, and of moral and political life as we know it. This transformation of our normal self-conception, which the truth of determinism would force upon us, is (according to Berlin) far more comprehensive and devastating than is usually believed by empiricist philosophers: in particular, it would encompass a mutation in our view of our own conduct that borders on the inconceivable. It is more than doubtful whether we have the capacity to throw off our phenomenological certainty of our own freedom as agents that are not wholly bound by natural causation and adopt the view of ourselves as natural objects or processes that is mandated by determinism. Internalizing the truth of determinism may well be a psychological impossibility – a point acknowledged in the most powerful recent statement of anti-compatibilist determinism.[7] According to Berlin, we have no reason to attempt this impossible feat, since there are no compelling arguments for human determinism; and our own experience, which proves so resistant to reconstruction on determinist lines, tells against it. The very universality and depth of the subjective conviction of free agency is an argument against human determinism, against which only the most powerful philosophical counter-argument could prevail. It is Berlin's view that no such compelling argument for determinism has yet been stated.

In this respect, Berlin, like Popper, holds that determinism is not even a necessary presupposition of the natural sciences.[8] In any event its falsity in the human world entails – what Berlin thinks plausible on independent grounds – that the human sciences cannot be built on the model, supposedly deterministic, of the natural sciences. There can in particular be no science of history: the project of a scientific history is broken-backed.[9] But there is in Berlin a deep difference from Popper, and from positivists of every variety, in that he rejects any form of methodological monism about inquiry, such as that which Popper advocates as the unity of the natural and social sciences,[10] and opts instead for methodological pluralism – the view that the methods of inquiry appropriate to different subject matters may, and do, vary with differences in these subject matters. The positivist ideal of a unified science, embracing all natural and social phenomena, is one Berlin has always repudiated. He rejects it in part because he sees it as an example of 'the desire to translate many prima facie different types of proposition into a single type' which is a recurring temptation of philosophers, and which he subjects to a powerful criticism in his early essay on 'Logical Translation'. There he rejects the positivistic project of reducing all propositions to a single type, arguing:

> To translate, reduce, deflate, is philosophically laudable so long as there is a real gain in clarity, simplicity, and the destruction of myths. But where it is obvious that types of proposition or sentence cannot be 'reduced' or 'translated' into one another without torturing the language until what was conveyed idiomatically before can no longer be conveyed so fully or clearly or, at times, at all in the artificial language constructed to conform to

some imaginary criterion of a 'logical perfection', such attempts should be exposed as stemming from a false theory of meaning, accompanied by its equally counterfeit metaphysical counterpart – a view of the universe as possessing an 'ultimate structure', as being constructed out of this or that collection or combination of bits and pieces of 'ultimate stuff' which the 'language' is constructed to reproduce.[11]

Berlin's thought is instructive, for this reason, in a way that (despite Popper's professed distance from the positivists of the Vienna Circle) Popper's is not, regarding the defects and limitations of positivism in philosophy.

Berlin's repudiation of determinism and compatibilism may seem to be at a considerable distance from his views in moral and political philosophy. It might even be maintained that nothing *follows* prescriptively from these metaphysical positions of Berlin's; and such a claim would not be altogether mistaken. There is nevertheless a coherence, if not perhaps any relations of logical entailment or of strict implication, between Berlin's opposition to human determinism and his account of moral and political life. The locus of this coherence is in the centrality Berlin accords to the activity of *choice* in the constitution of human nature. It must be noted at once that Berlin does not subscribe to the idea of a common human nature as that is found in Hobbes and in Locke, in Rousseau and even in Hume, in which a constant stock of unaltering needs, and a small set of human passions, are discerned behind the miscellany of cultural diversity in manners and mores, in self-understandings and conceptions of the good, that human history discloses to us. This is, at least in Locke and Rousseau, the idea of the 'natural man', denuded of the deceptive raiment of convention, whose character and needs are everywhere the same, before they are complicated or corrupted by the artefacts of civilization. Berlin does not subscribe to this notion of a common human nature, which goes back perhaps to the Sophists and

underlies classical as well as Christian accounts of natural
law, despite the fact that he is insistent that some conception of human nature is presupposed in every developed
moral and political theory. He affirms the indispensability
of a conception of man in our thought in his important paper
'Does Political Theory Still Exist?', where he observes: 'Our
conscious idea of man – of how men differ from other entities, of what is human and what is not human or inhuman
– involves the use of some among the basic categories in
terms of which we perceive and order and interpret data. To
analyse the concept of man is to recognize these categories
for what they are. To do this is to realize that they are
categories, that is, that they are not themselves subjects for
scientific hypotheses about the data which they order.'[12]
Here Berlin's argument follows those of philosophers such
as Hampshire and Strawson,[13] in setting as a task of philosophical inquiry the specification – via a sort of quasi-
Kantian transcendental deduction – of the necessary
'categories' of human agency. It is these categories, and not
any substantive claims about human motivations or interests, that give most of the content to the idea of human
nature in Berlin's account of it.

Berlin does not by human nature mean us to understand
any unvarying human passions or needs. Rather he takes
the capacity for choice, and for a self-chosen form of life, to
be itself constitutive of human beings, and to distinguish
them from other animal species, by introducing an element
of indeterminacy into their nature and conduct, which could
only be eradicated with the elimination of the capacity for
choice itself. If the capacity for choice introduces into
human nature this partial indeterminacy, if human understandings of human needs alter over time and in so doing
alter those very needs, then it will be in the capacity of
choice, with all the uncertainty and potential for novelty
that that carries with it, and not in any supposed range of
fixed universal needs, that the most distinctive mark of man
is to be found. It will indeed be the capacity of the human

species to invent for itself through the exercise of the powers of choice a diversity of natures, embodied in irreducibly distinct forms of life containing goods (and evils) that are sometimes incommensurable and so rationally incomparable, that constitutes the most distinctive mark of man. Berlin goes so far as to encapsulate this view by asserting that 'the necessity of choosing between absolute claims is then an inescapable characteristic of the human condition.'[14] It is clear that he believes that the capacity for choice he ascribes to the human species is originative and creative in a way that could not but be compromised by the truth of determinism.

The human capacity for choice supports Berlin's conception of freedom in that he designates as 'basic freedom' the capacity for choice itself – what Kant called *Willkür* – and affirms that this underpins both 'negative' and 'positive' liberty. Here Berlin seems to mean that even negative freedom – ordinarily understood, in the empiricist tradition, as noninterference by others when acting according to one's actual or potential desires – presupposes the capacity for choice among alternatives. An animal may be frustrated in doing what it wants by natural, or deliberately imposed, constraints on its behaviour; but unless it can envisage alternatives and in some sense choose between them it cannot be said to possess, or to lack, negative freedom in Berlin's sense. Negative freedom is not, then, the 'unimpeded motion' of Hobbes, nor the unobstructed pursuit of one's desires in terms of which it was conceived by Bentham, with which it is often identified, by such critics of Berlin as Charles Taylor.[15] It is rather *choice among alternatives or options that is unimpeded by others*. It cannot be ascribed to animals (at least on the conventional conception of their capacities), but nor could it have application to human beings who had been so conditioned that actions actually available to them could not be perceived by them as options – the majority of the inhabitants of *Brave New World*, for example. This is to say that Berlin's conception of 'basic freedom' as the availability of options is *not* the standard empiricist notion of liberty as action, unobstructed by others, according to actual or potential desires. An agent that never reflected on its desires, never evaluated them or deliberated about them, would on Berlin's account necessarily lack basic freedom. Lacking the capacity for choice among alternatives, such an agent could not possess negative freedom; such an agent could not even be denied negative freedom.

It will readily be seen that, if negative freedom as Berlin understands it presupposes the capacity for choice among alternatives, it shares a common root with positive freedom. Unlike negative freedom, which is the freedom from interference by others, positive freedom is the freedom of self-mastery, of rational control of one's life. It is plain that, as with negative freedom, positive freedom is impaired or diminished as the capacity or power of choice is impaired or diminished, but in different ways. An agent may be unobstructed in the choice of alternatives by other agents, and yet lack the ability or power to act. This may be because of negative factors, lacks or absences – of knowledge, money or other resources – or it may be because there are internal constraints, within the agent himself, preventing him from conceiving or perceiving alternatives as such, or else, even if they are so perceived, from acting on them. Such conditions as phobias or neurotic inhibitions may close off an agent's options, even to the point that they remain unknown to him, or else he may be constrained by irrational and invincible anxiety from acting so as to take advantage of them. In this case the power of choice has been sabotaged or compromised from within. An agent may possess very considerable negative freedom and yet, because he is incapacitated for choice among alternatives that others have not closed off from him, be positively unfree to an extreme degree. What both forms of unfreedom have in common is the restriction or incapacitation of the powers of choice.

Here several common misunderstandings of Berlin's account must be noted and discarded. Berlin is not advancing a linguistic, semantic or even conceptual analysis of the terms 'liberty' or 'freedom', after the fashion of Oxford ordinary-language philosophy in the 1950s. His conception of philosophical method is such that he would never suppose that philosophical puzzlement could be overcome by the analysis of the uses of words: his lifelong conviction that philosophical questions are *not* primarily linguistic in character is sufficient to show this. He states this view canonically when, in the course of arguing that there is a class of genuine philosophical questions that are neither empirical nor formal in character, he asserts: 'it seems clear that disagreements about the analysis of value concepts, as often as not, spring from profounder differences, since the notions of, say, rights or justice or liberty will be radically dissimilar for theists or atheists, mechanistic determinists and Christians, Hegelians and empiricists, romantic irrationalists and Marxists, and so forth. It seems no less clear that these differences are not, at least prima facie, either logical or empirical, and have usually and rightly been classified as irreducibly philosophical.' This statement, made in Berlin's seminal paper 'Does Political Theory Still Exist?',[16] establishes the distance between Berlin's conception of philosophical method and that, not only of the positivists, but also of linguistic philosophers, such as J. L. Austin. Along with many similar statements, it shows that for Berlin nothing decisive in philosophy ever turns on the meanings of words.

His argument is not, then, that 'liberty' *means* what he terms 'negative freedom' – non-interference by others in one's actual and potential chosen activities. Nor is he, for that and other reasons, maintaining that only negative freedom is *bona fide* freedom, or that it alone is valuable freedom. His theme, after all, is two concepts of freedom – two conceptions, one may say, in Rawls's idiom,[17] of the same thing. He is emphatic that 'positive and negative liberty are both perfectly valid concepts', that 'positive liberty . . . is essential to a decent existence'[18] and, in his early explicit statement of his view, he had already affirmed that the two ideas 'seem concepts at no great logical distance from each other – no more than negative or positive ways of saying much the same thing.' Yet, he continues, 'the "positive" and "negative" notions of freedom historically developed in divergent directions not always by logically reputable steps, until, in the end, they came into direct conflict with each other.'[19] Berlin's view, accordingly, is that negative and positive unfreedom have a common root in the denial or impairment of what Kant terms *Willkür* – the power of choice. Each embodies a valid conception of freedom, or even, it may be, a different aspect or dimension of the 'basic freedom' which *Willkür* designates. In historical terms, however, the two ideas of freedom have so developed that they now stand for distinct values, goods or conditions; so distinct are they, indeed, that they are often rivals or competitors in practice.

Berlin's insistence that these are two distinct, and often conflicting, conceptions of liberty, gives the lie to those of his critics who hold to formal conceptual analyses of the discourse of liberty according to which the distinction between the negative and positive views is merely semantic. This is the claim of McCallum,[20] for whom freedom is a triadic relation, into which both positive and negative views can be fitted, and for Feinberg, for whom it appears to be a tetradic concept, specifying four kinds of constraint on actions: external, internal, positive and negative.[21] Against McCallum, Berlin argues, soundly,[22] that the basic sense of liberty is dyadic, not triadic, since an agent may wish to be without a constraint, and yet have no specific action he wishes then to perform: so that the formal schema McCallum proposes for the discourse of liberty – agent *a* is free from constraint *b* to perform action *c* – does not capture the most primitive root of the idea of freedom, which is simply the rejection of constraints imposed by others, merely as such. Against Feinberg, Berlin could argue forcefully that the tetradic schema is far too copious, allowing as constraints *on freedom* constraints and evils (such as headaches, disabilities) that are not unfreedoms at all. The trouble with this schema of Feinberg's, in other words, is that it allows virtually every good and evil that can constrain human conduct to be translatable into the discourse of liberty. This is far too permissive a schema, and one that violates Bishop Butler's dictum (often cited by Berlin) that 'Things and actions are what they are, and their consequences will be what they will be: why then should we seek to be deceived?' The effect of Feinberg's, and similar analyses, is to obliterate freedom as a distinct political value.

In a famous statement, Berlin has asserted that 'The fundamental sense of freedom is freedom from chains, from imprisonment, from enslavement by others. The rest is an extension of this sense, or else metaphor.'[23] Here Berlin is arguing, not that this sense of freedom alone conforms with ordinary usage or linguistic intuition, but rather that it is in the restriction of choice among alternatives by other human agents that the most fundamental unfreedom is to be found. In part his reason for holding this view is that he is concerned with freedom *inter homines*, with civil or social or political freedom, not with the 'freedom' men may find in submission to the will of God, to the Categorical Imperative or (if they are Stoics) in identification with the natural or rational order. More radically, he rejects the rationalist and monist presuppositions and doctrines with which ideas of positive freedom have become associated in the history of philosophy. For Berlin, freedom, even positive freedom, always connotes choice, never the recognition of necessity. It would be hard to find a view of freedom more alien to Berlin's than that adumbrated in Spinoza's *Ethics*. Yet even Spinoza's conception of freedom as the individual recognition of necessity has an advantage, from Berlin's standpoint, over later positive conceptions, such as Hegel's, in that it sees positive freedom as *individual* self-determination, not collective self-rule. The nemesis of positive freedom, the moment when it is transformed from a genuine – if, in the end, for reasons I try to specify below, for Berlin a philosophically indefensible – conception of freedom into a pseudo-conception, a version of another value that masquerades as freedom, comes when it designates the integration of a community in harmonious self-government. It is this nemesis which came to pass, according to Berlin, in such German Idealists as Fichte and Hegel.

It must be confessed that there seems to be a difficulty in Berlin's account here, since the conceptions of positive freedom as rational self-direction by the individual, and as harmonious collective self-determination, were themselves indissolubly conjoined in the positive conception of freedom attributed to the Greeks by Benjamin Constant in his 'Liberty Ancient and Modern', to which Berlin has acknowledged his indebtedness.[24] It seems that the most offensive feature of positive freedom, its conflation of individual self-direction with collective self-rule, was present from the start, in the ancient Greek view of it. It is difficult then for Berlin to maintain that later conceptions of positive freedom as collective self-rule are perversions of earlier, and more legitimate, conceptions of it as individual self-determination. Constant seems on firmer ground in holding that the ancient or positive sense of freedom *was* that of collective self-rule, and that the negative conception is distinctively modern.

There is a further difficulty in that, though the negative conception seems to be distinctively modern, it does not appear to be distinctively liberal. Two of its most uncompromising exponents – Hobbes and Bentham – were not liberals, and many liberals, such as Kant and J. S. Mill, have held to positive conceptions of liberty as autonomy. That Kant's conception of individual freedom was one of rational autonomy is recognized by Berlin himself;[25] and the fact that J. S. Mill's was a similar conception is shown in the fact that the subject of *On Liberty* is not the restraint of negative liberty by legal coercion but the curbing of individual autonomy by the 'moral coercion' of an invasive public opinion. As the examples of these two seminal liberal thinkers demonstrate, there is certainly no necessary connection between the negative view of liberty and liberalism. The connection is established, in Berlin's own liberalism, by an account of the value of negative liberty, not – as in Hobbes and Bentham – primarily as a means to want-satisfaction, but as a condition of self-creation through choice-making. It is Berlin's explanation of the *value* of negative freedom, in other words, that is meant to assure to this distinctively modern conception a liberal content. It is not Berlin's view, however, that the negative view of liberty has any unique or constitutive place in the liberal tradition; such a view would not stand up to historical scrutiny. Berlin's view seems to be, rather, that the liberal tradition is itself complex and indeed pluralistic in character, and accommodates many conceptions of freedom; but that the negative one is most defensible, and most congenial to liberal concerns with diversity and toleration, in so far as it in no way rests upon the rationalist and monist doctrines associated with the positive view.

In other words, this apparent difficulty in Berlin's account of the historical development of the two ideas gives a clue to his most fundamental reason for *rejecting* positive freedom as the most adequate conception of freedom. This is in Berlin's attribution to the positive view of a rationalist and monist conception of the good. According to Berlin, in the positive view, whether it be Socratic or Stoic, Spinozistic or Kantian, Hegelian or Fichtean, freedom consists not in choice but in obedience to rational will. Whereas choice presupposes genuine rivalry among conflicting goods, rational will points to one, and only one course of action, one form of life, for the individual. Further, in Plato, as in Socrates and Aristotle, the rational will for each person is the same as that for every person: they have the same object, itself the same for all. So, just as there is for each agent a form of life that is uniquely rational for him, so every agent will converge on that very form of life, since it is the same for all. It may well be that the empirical selves of actual men and women are riddled with conflicting goals and desires, plagued by rivalries among cherished goods and values, and that these conflicts are only compounded in the relations between agents; but the rational will, once it is oriented towards the order of nature or the Form of the Good, cannot contain such conflicts, since these betoken unreason and even unreality. Freedom for agents so conceived is not in choice among genuinely rivalrous alternatives, but in pursuing and adopting what is rational or right. It is in cleaving to the true and the good, which are one and the same, for each and all, that freedom is exercised.

It is in the implication for this view for political practice that Berlin finds the most objectionable and dangerous features of positive freedom. For if genuine freedom is the opportunity to pursue the good, if all true goods are compatible with one another and are indeed the same for all persons, then a community of truly free persons will be one without significant conflict of values, ideals or interests, a harmonious dovetailing of identical real or rational wills. This was, presumably, Rousseau's vision of the General Will. It is a perilously illiberal vision, since its implication is that all moral, social or political conflict is a symptom of immorality or unreason, or, at the very least, of error. The deepest monist presupposition of this view is that there must of necessity be an identity of wills among free men, such that they constitute – at least ideally – a conflictless community. This is the presupposition, with its diagnosis of conflict as inherently pathological, which, in Berlin's view, underpins all forms of totalitarianism from the Jacobins to our own day. Further, if – as he thinks – this monist view is itself inherent in positive conceptions of freedom, then they are inherently liable to abuse, on account of this flaw, and not, as with negative freedom and all genuine political ideals, contingently susceptible to misuse in practice.

It is Berlin's rejection of this monist vision, his pluralist insistence on the diversity and incommensurability of genuine human goods, that is his *idée maîtresse*. It is also the animating idea of his account of freedom. Negative freedom is to be commended and adopted as the fundamental species of freedom because it is most consistent with the rivalrous diversity of human purposes and goods. Positive freedom, though it designates an authentic species of freedom, that in which it concerns self-mastery, easily, and according to Berlin inevitably, degenerates into the fantasy of ethical rationalism, which is fatal to choice. (It may even have begun in such a fantasy, in the Platonistic or Socratic doctrine of the Form of the Good, and the Aristotelian doctrine of the unity of the virtues.) For the self which is master of itself is rarely, in positive accounts of freedom, the actual empirical self, with all its idiosyncrasy, embarrassments and lacunae, it is typically an abstract self, an exemplar of rational humanity, indistinguishable from any other. In this view the root of freedom in the differences among agents, and in the conflicts among the goods they pursue, has vanished.

The nature and grounds of Berlin's pluralism are the subject of the next chapter. At this point a feature of his thought, to which I shall recur at the end of this book, is worthy of note. I have pointed out that there is in Berlin no account of a common human nature that is universal and the same for all, since the propensity to diversity, to difference, is itself implied by the human capacity for choice. It is not that commonality is natural, difference artificial or conventional; rather, diversity is the most evident expression of man's nature as a species whose life is characterized by choice. Such choice is, for Berlin, choice among goods that are not only distinct and rivalrous but sometimes incommensurable: it is radical choice, ungoverned by reason. It is, *in extremis*, the choice of a nature in the self-creation of an individual, or the collective creation of a form of life. Human nature is not, for Berlin, something within us all that awaits discovery and realization. It is something invented, and perpetually reinvented, through choice, and it is inherently plural and diverse, not common or universal.

A question arises at this point about the status of this conception of man as a self-transforming being and its relations with Berlin's moral and political theory. What are the epistemological credentials of this conception of man, and how is it to be assessed? How, if at all, is it related to the celebration of choice-making which is a distinctive feature of Berlin's liberalism? In answer to the first question, it would seem that the conception of man as a species that transforms itself through choice-making is grounded partly in the evidences of cultural difference afforded by history. What history discloses is not a stable human nature subject to minor variations, but an extraordinarily inventive species with a plethora of cultural identities. To affirm, as Berlin does, that the self-transformation of human nature occurs through the human exercise of the powers of choice is not to say that its changes are the results of premeditated intentions; it is to say that they are expressions of the human capacity for choice, which cannot be captured in any deterministic schema of explanation. This latter claim trades on Berlin's arguments against human determinism, and testifies to the presence of an a priori element in his conception of man – one, that is to say, that is supported by philosophical reasonings rather than by historical or other empirical evidences. The epistemological basis of Berlin's conception of man as a being in whose nature choice-making is central is, then, partly philosophical and partly historical. It should be clear – if only because to think otherwise would be to commit a fallacy of ethical naturalism – that the truth of this conception of man would not guarantee the acceptability of a form of liberalism in which the exercise of the powers of choice is accorded a central place in the human good. The conception of the good life as the chosen life is a highly culturally specific one, which must be supported, if it can be supported, by considerations other than those Berlin invokes in support of his general conception of man. Indeed it could be objected against Berlin's account that what it shows is *not* the centrality of choice-making in human nature but simply its variability and its propensity to cultural difference – very different things. I will maintain in the final chapter of this book that this criticism is not altogether warranted, since at least some forms of cultural difference arise from choices among incommensurable values. It is, however, worth remarking here on an insight suggested by such a line of criticism – that the conception of human nature as only partly determinate and accordingly culturally variable to a significant degree, which is true universally if it is true at all, is a very different animal from the conception of man as a species whose most distinctive activity, and the activity which is the precondition of all that is most valuable in human life, is the making of choices. This conception of man accords with the self-understanding of practitioners of certain modern, Western cultural traditions, but it in no way follows from the idea of man as a self-transforming being.

The forms of life in which human beings constitute for themselves a diversity of natures are many and variable, and they embody values that are irreducibly different and on occasion incommensurable. They are also often conflicting and uncombinable. One conclusion drawn from this deep conflict of values between and among divergent forms of life in what I have called Berlin's agonistic liberalism is that there can be no overarching principle of liberty, and no structure of fundamental rights or set of basic liberties, fixed or determinate in their content and harmonious or dovetailing in their scope. Rather conflict and rivalry enter into the ideal of liberty itself, as our liberties disclose themselves to be rivalrous and incommensurable values between which we must choose, without the benefit of any overarching rational standard.

It follows from Berlin's view of negative liberty as being itself composed of a diversity of often conflicting and sometimes incommensurable liberties that there can be no *theory* or *principle* which determines how these conflicts are to be resolved. Indeed, because negative liberties may be incommensurably valuable, there can be no theory, or libertarian calculus, which tells us when negative liberty is maximized. As Berlin has put this latter point, in an important and often neglected passage:

> 'Negative liberty' is something the extent of which, in a given case, it is difficult to estimate . . . The extent of my freedom seems to depend on a) how many possibilities are open to me (though the method of counting these can never be more than impressionistic. Possibilities of action are not discrete entities like apples, which can be exhaustively enumerated; b) how easy or difficult each of these possibilities is to actualize; c) how important in my plan of life, given my character and circumstances, these possibilities are when compared with each other; d) how far they are closed and opened by deliberate human acts; e) what value not merely the agent, but the general sentiment of the society in which he lives, puts on the various possibilities. All these magnitudes must be 'integrated', and a conclusion, necessarily never precise, or indisputable, drawn from this process. It may well be that there are many incommensurable kinds and degrees of freedom, and that they cannot be drawn up on any single scale of magnitude.[26]

Here Berlin's argument is that judgements of comparative or on-balance freedom (in this case negative freedom) are themselves evaluative judgements; they are not value-free or value-neutral assessments of states of affairs in the human world upon which agreement can be reached even among those whose value-judgements are divergent. Indeed, his point is that even people who acknowledge the same goods or values will make different judgements of on-balance freedom, in so far as they attach different weightings to liberties that are incommensurable in their value.

Two further points, which may prove of considerable importance, flow from Berlin's recognition of incommensurabilities within negative liberty itself, and from his account of the variety of ways in which it may be restricted. The first is that he does not consider negative liberty to be an 'absolute' value which is not to be put in the balance with others. For this reason, he does not accept the unconditional priority of liberty over other political values that is affirmed in the Kantian liberalism of John Rawls, insisting instead that trade-offs between liberty and other values are often legitimate and indeed unavoidable. Berlin's view that there can be no *principle* which tells us how to make trade-offs between negative liberty and other values when these are incommensurables raises questions as to the relations of his value-pluralism with his liberalism to which I will return repeatedly in the course of my interpretation of his thought.

The second point is that his account of the various dimensions in terms of which negative freedom may be curbed or restricted shows that he does not think it is limited only by force or coercion. The range of factors by which someone's negative freedom may in Berlin's account be restrained is considerably larger. Indeed in other places in his writings[27] he is explicit that negative unfreedom, the obstruction of agents' choices by others, need not presuppose the deliberate interference by others which occurs when force or coercion is deployed, but only the reasonable attribution of human responsibility for the unintended consequences of human action. Negative freedom may thus be diminished by acts of omission as well as by deliberate interventions: what is required for negative freedom to be at stake is not intention but instead the alterability of social states and human responsibility for them. Further, Berlin is explicit that a social theory is required, specifying the alterability of social arrangements and the causes for their being as they are, whenever we make judgements about negative freedom of this broader sort. As he puts it, programmatically: 'If my lack of material means is due to my lack of mental or physical capacity, then I begin to speak of being deprived of freedom (and not simply of poverty) only if I accept the theory (of its social causes and of human responsibility for their being as they are) . . . The criterion of oppression is the part that I believe to be played by other human beings, directly or indirectly, with or without the intention of doing so, in frustrating my wishes.'[28] Judgements about negative freedom are not, then, either value-neutral or theory-neutral. On the contrary, in Berlin's account, they are value-judgements, often involving incommensurabilities, and they depend on theoretical claims, often, no doubt, intractably controversial claims. Negative freedom remains choice among alternatives or options that is not impeded or obstructed by others; but what counts as an impediment or an obstruction will often be disputable, and is never a simple matter of fact. It is worth making these points, if only to mark the deep and sharp contrast between Berlin's conception of negative liberty and that of positivists such as Oppenheim,[29] who aspire to a language of freedom that is purged of evaluative connotations and of controversial theoretical claims. Nothing could be further from Berlin's account of freedom than such a positivistic conception.

We have not, as yet, considered in any extended way Berlin's account of the value or worth of freedom, negative or positive. It should be clear, from what has been said thus far about his views, that he cannot conceive the value of freedom in standard Anglo-American fashion, empiricist or utilitarian, as a means to want-satisfaction. Statements abound in his writings to the effect that freedom is an intrinsic good, an ultimate value, not merely a means to the satisfaction of human desires.[30] But in what does the good of freedom, particularly negative freedom, consist, if not in its facilitating the satisfaction of wants, or, at any rate, in avoiding the frustration of want-satisfaction by other agents? Joseph Raz, in the most profound consideration of these issues in recent philosophy since Berlin's,[31] proposes that the chief value of negative freedom is in its contribution to the positive freedom of autonomy. Here Raz does not mean that the negative freedom of non-interference is a necessary precondition of autonomy, in the sense of being a useful means to it; rather it is a constitutive ingredient of autonomous agency that one not be subject to the will of others. For Raz, however, non-interference is only one aspect of autonomy, which comprehends much else, including capacities for rational deliberation, the possession of adequate resources for meaningful action, and an array of worthwhile options from which to choose. It is autonomy, and not negative freedom, which has for Raz the status of an intrinsic good, and all, or most of, the value of negative freedom is in its enhancement of autonomy.

Raz's argument is of great subtlety and profundity, yet it is clear that it is not acceptable to Berlin. For one thing, the intrinsic value of freedom, especially of negative freedom, is in its embodiment of the 'basic freedom' of choice itself – not the rational choice among genuine goods and worthwhile options that is designated by autonomy, but choice *simpliciter*. Such choice may be capricious or whimsical, perverse or unreasonable, quixotic or self-destructive: it remains choice, and, as such, the source of the value of negative freedom (as well as of positive freedom in its genuine conceptions). The danger of Raz's account, from Berlin's viewpoint, is that it confines the value of freedom to the rational adoption of worthwhile ends. This aspect of Raz's liberalism flows almost inexorably from its 'perfectionist' character – that is to say, from the fact that its constitutive morality is one in which an ideal of human character and a conception of the good life are central. For Raz's liberalism, freedom is valuable only in so far as it makes a contribution to the good life, conceived in terms of the rational pursuit of choiceworthy options. Raz's liberalism thereby comes perilously close to the assimilation of freedom with reason or with virtue that Berlin finds to be a fatal flaw in most positive conceptions of freedom.

It may be that conceptions of autonomy may be more or less open or closed, in so far as they allow of more or less genuine choice among goods and forms of life; but it seems that all must link autonomous choice with the rational

pursuit of the good. It is the restriction of individual freedom to this form of life that Berlin rejects. Berlin's view
cuts against that of Raz in another way. It seems that in Raz
the ground of freedom and toleration is in competitive moral
pluralism – in the irreducible diversity of incommensurable
goods. Some of these goods are constitutively uncombinable;[32] they cannot be conjoined in a single person or a
single life. A regime of freedom and toleration is mandated,
accordingly, since it allows for a diversity of human
flourishings wider than any that could be accommodated
within one human life, or within a society governed by a
single conception of the good. It is clear that this argument
of Raz's touches Berlin's at many points.

It diverges from Berlin's, nevertheless, at the most crucial
points. For the pluralism sheltered under a regime of liberty,
in Raz's account of it, is a pluralism of *goods*, of valuable
forms of life and worthwhile options. It does not – except
as a concession to human fallibility – encompass evils, or
forms of life of little or no intrinsic worth. In Raz's account,
indeed, the value of autonomy appears to be itself problematical. In his view, autonomy is a necessary ingredient of
the good forms of life accessible to agents who live in cultural and historical milieux such as our own – milieux that
are highly mobile and discursive, which demand skills in
deliberative reasoning and reflective choice-making, that are
highly changeable, and so on. On Raz's account, then, the
value of autonomy is contextual, as an ingredient in the
forms of human flourishing that are feasible in certain definite historical and cultural contexts, such as our own. It is
not autonomous choice, still less choice itself, that is valuable on Raz's account, but instead the life that is chosen.
The autonomous choice of a worthless life, if such there can
be, is valueless even though it *is* autonomous. Raz's view
of the relations of autonomous choice with the good life
seems to be genuinely Aristotelian in that autonomous
choice, though it enters into many forms of human flourishing and excellence as a necessary ingredient, has value only

when it is a component of a form of life or activity that has itself intrinsic value. To this extent, the value of autonomy, for Raz as for Aristotle, is more instrumental than it is intrinsic.

Berlin does not deny that autonomy is a good, even perhaps an intrinsic good, if a far more problematical one than is dreamt of in Kantian philosophy; but he denies that the goodness of negative freedom is derivative from that of autonomy. This does not mean that the goodness of negative freedom derives from its contribution to want-satisfaction, as I myself supposed when I endorsed Raz's alternative account of its value as a constituent of autonomy;[33] for Berlin's is the very different view that negative freedom is valuable primarily as a condition of self-creation through choice-making. Berlin's insight here is the profound one that, since an autonomous subject is only one of the sorts of selves that can be created through choice-making, it is self-creation and not autonomy that gives value to negative freedom. Nor is there in Berlin's thought anything akin to the Aristotelian view, to which Raz seems to hold, that the value of choice-making is as a means to human flourishing. The goodness of negative freedom is for Berlin in the fact that it is expressive of choice, and the goodness of choice is in the fact that we are creatures who are part creators of themselves, and part authors of their lives, through the choices they make. Whether this account of the value of negative freedom really grounds a liberal political morality in which the promotion of negative liberty has pre-eminence is an issue to which I shall have to recur again and again. At this stage in my exposition and argument, it is worth observing that the difference between the view of the role of choice in Berlin's account of the value of negative freedom and in Raz's conception of autonomy may seem a fine one, but it remains of crucial importance. For the pluralism that negative freedom licenses is not a pluralism of goods alone: it accommodates a pluralism of the bad and the worthless, in that it affirms the freedom to choose that which is not, in the end, choiceworthy. For Berlin, accordingly, negative freedom has intrinsic value, even when it does not issue in autonomy, or the choice of the good. It has value, even in this case, because it is a condition of self-creation.

Here Berlin's view reveals its affinities with that of the Romantics, along with the idea of *Bildung* deployed by German classical liberals such as von Humboldt, and later adopted by J. S. Mill. It differs from the liberalism of Humboldt and J. S. Mill in that the latter are perfectionist: the value of choice in Humboldt and in Mill derives from its essential role in 'unfolding' the unique potentialities, or nature, of the individual self. Berlin, however, rejects any 'essentialist' conception of the self in which it has an individual nature, or quiddity,[34] which choice discloses. For Berlin, selfhood is a matter of invention rather than of the discovery of an individual nature, and the self-creation that occurs in choice-making is not the embodiment of an essential identity. Berlin's rejection of the idea of an essential individual self that is discovered through choice-making makes his conception of self-creation more radically voluntaristic than that of liberals, such as J. S. Mill, who were influenced by Romanticism. It also makes Berlin's liberalism anti-perfectionist, but without the apparatus of moral neutrality and of Kantian subjecthood that supports anti-perfectionism in the liberalism of Rawls or Dworkin. This is a point to which I will return, but it is worth remarking on here as an area of deep divergence between Berlin and Raz.

Unlike Raz's, Berlin's liberalism is not grounded in the ideal of autonomy, even if he is ready to grant that autonomy is a good. Such autonomy-based liberalism, from Berlin's standpoint, elevates a controversial and questionable ideal of life uncritically and unduly. There are many excellent lives that are not especially autonomous, and which liberal societies can shelter: the life of the nun, of the professional soldier, or the artist passionately devoted to his work, may be lives in which rare and precious goods are embodied, and

yet lives that are, in very different ways, far from autonomous. The idea which the 'basic freedom' of choice-making
supports is not that of autonomy, but of self-creation, where
the self that is created may very well *not* be that of an
autonomous agent. To demand of self-creation that it conform with an ideal of rational autonomy is, for Berlin as
for other liberals, such as Lomasky,[35] an unacceptably and
unnecessarily restrictive requirement. It excludes the life of
the traditionalist, whose choices confirm a self-identity that
has been inherited, as much as those of the mystic, or the
playful hedonist, for whom a fixed identity may be a useless
encumbrance, and the reflective deliberation that is
involved in autonomous agency a burdensome distraction.
Berlin's liberalism is here radically different from the *auton-
omist liberalism* of which Raz's is the best exemplar. His
claim that it is negative liberty, not autonomy, that is the
primordial or fundamental sense of freedom, expresses, as
much as anything else, his belief that the pluralism it allows
of forms of self-creation is more copious and populous than
that which is circumscribed by the ideal of rational autonomy. It is at this fundamental point, among others, that
Berlin's and Raz's variants of ethical pluralism diverge in
their implications for liberty.

There is a further argument against rational autonomy in
Berlin which is worth mentioning here, and to which I shall
recur. This is his argument that, for a single individual,
valued goods and projects may not be reconcilable in a harmonious individuality: the individual my be compelled, in
virtue of the constitutive uncombinability of distinct goods,
virtues, excellences and projects, to renounce some for the
sake of others, in the full knowledge that this renunciation
entails an irreparable loss of value, and that no principle can
be invoked which could settle the conflict within his life by
practical reasoning. The individual agent may be compelled
to choose between uncombinable goods and virtues, where
the choice is a radical choice between incommensurables.
The situation is yet harder than this. The pursuit of the ideal

of autonomy, if that involves the increase of self-knowledge, may issue in a weakening or destruction of personal powers that depend for their vitality or existence on repression, on blockages in self-knowledge. This is Berlin's argument in his important and neglected paper, 'From Hope and Fear Set Free',[36] in which he conjectures that great artistic gifts – the gifts of Van Gogh or Dostoyevsky, say – may be dependent on flaws in self-knowledge and may be destroyed, or impaired, by an enhancement of self-knowledge. A successful psychoanalyst might have turned Van Gogh into a contented bourgeois; it is unlikely that it would have left him with the power to paint as he did. It is not only that the ideal of autonomy crowds out other ideals of life, then, but that it may be self-limiting in the individual case as well. The pursuit of autonomy through enhanced self-knowledge may deplete in a person powers and capacities that are centrally constitutive of the self his choices have created, that are necessary for the pursuit of projects by which that self is defined, and which are recognized by others as essential for the accomplishment of intrinsically valuable activities. This must be so, indeed, if our individual natures may contain conflicts and contradictions, such that our personal powers cannot be augmented across the board. It may well be, for example, that profound self-knowledge is in many people an impediment to the vitality required in successful practical action, or to the intensity of vision needed in artistic creativity; it may even be true of many people that the examined life is not worth living. For many people, perhaps for all, the all-round development of the powers of autonomous agency may be an impossibility. It is just this possibility – or, as I would myself say, this commonplace fact – that the ideal of autonomy, like the Millian ideal of rounded or harmonious individuality, neglects, and which Berlin seeks to recall to our attention.

Both Berlin and Raz are value-pluralists in that they assert an irreducible diversity of incommensurable goods. Both affirm that the goods of human life are rivalrous and uncombinable, in many cases, and that not all can be achieved harmoniously, if at all, in a single human life. Berlin's value-pluralism may diverge from Raz's, however, in holding that goods may depend upon, or presuppose, evils, and right actions contain, or entail, wrongs. It is this darker version of value-pluralism that gives Berlin's liberalism its agonistic character and that motivates his ambivalence towards, indeed his resistance to, ideals of rational autonomy. If many forms of life and conceptions of the good are not combinable with autonomous agency, but are nevertheless ways in which human beings may freely engage in self-creation through choice-making, if the pursuit of autonomy even in the individual case may result in an impoverishment of personal powers when these are undermined by the critical reflexivity and self-knowledge that autonomy presupposes, then autonomy – though it may be an ideal that some find compelling, and which a liberal society should shelter – cannot be the foundation of a liberal political morality. Berlin's liberalism diverges radically from J. S. Mill's, accordingly, in that ideals of autonomy and individuality are neither central nor fundamental in it.

In this respect, though in very few others, Berlin's liberalism is akin to the 'political liberalism'[37] of the later Rawls in refusing to ground liberal practice in a comprehensive ideal such as that of autonomy, and diverges from any strongly perfectionist liberalism such as Raz's. It repudiates perfectionism, however, not by reference to a questionable, and (as Raz has shown)[38] dubiously coherent ideal of neutrality, of the sort that is found in the liberalism of Rawls and Dworkin, but by pointing to the diversity of worthwhile lives that are not autonomous (but which may yet be self-chosen). Berlin's liberalism is significant in that its anti-perfectionism is *not* grounded in any Kantian idea of the priority of the right over the good of the sort that is found in the work of Rawls and Dworkin. In this connection Berlin is at one with Raz in rejecting any such Kantian view in which deontic considerations are foundational in morality.

In particular, he is at one with Raz in the view that political morality is not, and cannot be, rights-based.[39] It cannot be rights-based, for Berlin as for Raz, inasmuch as both the grounds and the contents of human rights can only be spelt out in terms of their contribution to the human good. His position differs radically from that of Raz, however, in that it is not founded on any Aristotelian view of flourishing as the bottom line in ethics, and it attaches no central importance to autonomy. Berlin's anti-perfectionism derives instead from his value-pluralism, with its explicit recognition of the diversity of worthwhile lives that goes well beyond those that can be lived by the autonomous subject of liberal theory. Or, to put the same point in other words, if Berlin's ethical theory is to be cashed out in terms of a conception of human flourishing, it is one that is radically unAristotelian in its assertion of the irreducible plurality and incommensurability of the forms of human flourishing, arising from a thoroughly unAristotelian account of the irreducible plurality of human natures that are constituted through choice-making.[40]

One may say that, for Berlin, the justification of a liberal society cannot be primarily that it harbours liberal individuals (in Gauthier's sense),[41] that is to say, autonomous subjects having all the powers and capacities that autonomy implies, but rather that it permits a far greater variety of forms of self-creation through choice-making. Berlin's preference for negative liberty over autonomy is motivated by this latter fact, together with the fact that negative liberty allows for individual choice among incommensurable evils as well as among incommensurable goods. It allows, more particularly, for choices in which particular combinations of incommensurable goods presuppose, or contain among their preconditions, particular combinations of incommensurable evils. Most especially, the negative conception of liberty allows individuals to engage in forms of self-creation in which autonomy does not figure, which autonomy might undermine, or which develop some dimensions of autonomy

at the expense of other, uncombinable and perhaps incommensurable dimensions of it.[42] A question arises for Berlin
as to why, if he attaches no central importance to autonomy
or to the liberal individual, he should seek to privilege negative freedom among ultimate values. If ultimate values are
incommensurable, and no ranking among them is uniquely
rational, or more rational than any other, what could warrant giving special weight to negative freedom? This is an
especially hard question for Berlin, when we consider that
self-creation through choice-making occurs in his account
of it at the collective as well as the individual level – and
when it is noted that the creation of collective identities,
even more than self-creation through individual choice,
often involves imposing restraints on negative freedom. It
is harder yet for Berlin when we consider that the self that
is created and renewed through choice-making may not only
not be the autonomous subject or liberal individual; it may
be a self whose identity is constituted by participation in
a form of life that is not liberal.[43] It is accordingly to the
value-pluralism that Berlin's conception of negative freedom
invokes, and to its complex relations with liberalism in any
of the latter's varieties, that I now turn.

2 Pluralism

What is the best life for men? And, more particularly, what
is the most perfect society? There is, after all, no dearth
of solutions. Every age has provided its own formulas. Some
have looked for the solution in sacred books or in
revelation or in the words of inspired prophets or the
tradition of organized priesthoods; others found it in the
rational insight of the skilled metaphysician, or in the
combination of scientific observation and experiment, or in
the 'natural' good sense of men not 'scribbled over' by
philosophers or theologians or perverted by 'interested
error'. Still others have found it only in the uncorrupted
heart of the simple good man. Some thought that only trained
experts could discover great and saving truths; others
supposed that on questions of value all sane men were
equally well qualified to judge. Some maintained that such
truths could be discovered at any time, and that it was mere
bad luck that it had taken so long to find the most important
among them, or that they had been so easily forgotten. Others
held that mankind was subject to the law of growth; and
that the truth would not be seen in its fullness until
mankind had reached maturity – the age of reason. Some
doubted even this, and said men could never attain to such
knowledge on earth; or if they did were too weak to follow
it in practice, since such perfection was attainable only by
angels, or in the life hereafter. But one assumption was
common to all these views: it was, at any rate in principle,
possible to draw some outline of the perfect society or the
perfect man, if only to define how far a given society or a
given individual fell short of the ideal. This was necessary
if one was to be able to compare degrees of imperfection. But
this belief in the final objective answer had not been
absolutely universal. Relativists held that different
circumstances and temperaments demanded different

policies; but, for the most part, even they supposed that, though routes might differ, the ultimate goal – human happiness, the satisfaction of human wishes – was one and the same. Some sceptical thinkers in the ancient world – Carneades, for example – went further and uttered the disquieting thought that some ultimate values might be incompatible with one another, so that no solution could logically incorporate them all. There was something of this doubt about the logic of the concept of the perfect society not only among the Greeks, but in the Renaissance too, in Pontano, in Montaigne, in Machiavelli, and after them in Leibniz and Rousseau, who thought that no gain could be made without a corresponding loss. Something of this, too, seemed to lie at the heart of the tragedies of Sophocles, Euripides, and Shakespeare. Nevertheless, the central stream of the Western tradition was little affected by this fundamental doubt. The central assumption was that problems of value were in principle soluble, and soluble with finality. Whether the solution could be implemented by imperfect men was another question, a question which did not affect the rationality of the universe. This is the keystone of the classical arch, which, after Herder, began to crumble.

Isaiah Berlin, 'Herder and the Enlightenment'[1]

At the very beginnings of the Western intellectual tradition it is affirmed that all genuine goods are compatible. In the Platonic conception of the Form of the Good, yet more is affirmed: that all genuine goods are not only compatible with one another – that is to say, in ideal circumstances, conjointly realizable, achievable together – but that they somehow entail or imply one another. The same idea, more moderately expressed, is found in the Aristotelian ideas of the Mean and of the unity of the virtues – the idea, in this case, that no true excellence or mode of human flourishing can, at any rate in the best human life, compete with, or drive out, any other. In Aristotle's case this monist conception of the virtues is supported by an account of practical reasoning that has dominated Western philosophy until modern times. As Alasdair MacIntyre states this Aristotelian view:

> There is . . . [a] feature of Aristotle's conception of practical rationality that is . . . at odds with a dominant modern conception. On a characteristically modern view the claims upon particular individuals of some good may be inconsistent with the claims of some other good, thus creating dilemmas for which on occasion there may be no mode of rational solution. Precisely because Aristotle's logic in practical argument is the same deductive logic employed in theoretical argument, and precisely because there can only be at any one time one right action to perform, the premises of any Aristotelian practical argument must be consistent with all other truths. It cannot be true of someone on Aristotle's view that he or she is required by the claims upon him or her of some good to do such and such and by the claims of some other equal or incommensurable good not to do such and such. The difference between Aristotle and the modern view is perhaps most clearly apparent in the different interpretations of tragedy which each engenders. From the modern standpoint the incompatibility between the demands of one good and those of another can be real, and it is in terms of the reality of such dilemmas that tragedy is to be understood. It *can* therefore be held to be true of someone that he or she should do such and such (because one good requires it) and also that he or she should refrain from doing such and such (because some other good requires such refraining). But if these both can be held to be true, the concept of truth has been transformed; this is not truth as transmitted by valid deductive arguments. It is for this very reason that from Aristotle's point of view the apparent existence of a tragic dilemma must always rest upon one or more misconceptions or misunderstandings. The apparent and tragic conflict of right with right

arises from the inadequacies of reason, not from the character of moral reality.[2]

Aristotle's account of practical reason was not an aberrant one among the Greeks; it was apparently held by Socrates, and indeed by all major Greek philosophers, apart perhaps from a few Sophists. In so far as MacIntyre appears to deny that the ideas of deep value conflict and of radical choice, such as are captured in the notion of incommensurability, are lacking in the ancient Greek world, he is probably mistaken, given the Sophist examples to the contrary cited by Berlin. His claim that the modern conception of ethics and of practical reasoning is marked by any such ideas is equally disputable, since that conception is typically sceptical and subjectivist, not objectively pluralist. This is to say that the most distinctive feature of the modern view of ethics is found in the denial of moral knowledge, in the rejection of anything akin to moral belief or moral judgement, and in the consequent assimilation of morality to the expression of preference. This is in sharp contrast with Berlin's objective pluralism, which insists that values and conflicts of value are matters of knowledge for us, with the necessity of radical choice arising only in conflicts of incommensurables. This objective pluralist view is almost as unfamiliar and uncommon in modern times as it is in the ancient world. Aristotle's view of ethics is the standard Greek view in that it represents moral reasoning as a sort of practical syllogism, in which true premises are bound to yield correct moral judgements (or acts) as their conclusions; and it entails that right action cannot contain wrong. These are features of Greek ethics, not indeed as it is found in Homer, but throughout the tradition that takes Socrates as its point of departure. Behind such doubtful affirmations lies a conception of rationality, according to which every genuine question must have, at least in principle, a single right answer. So, to the question – undoubtedly a genuine enough one – 'Shall I pursue the good of knowledge, or the good of beauty?'

– this view of reason, aboriginal among the Greeks and deep-seated among the Romans, implies that there can be only one genuine answer. It implies this, in part, because it typically presupposes that there cannot be competition or conflict among genuine goods, so that the answer to any such question would be bound to be 'Both', or else one that denies the genuineness of one of the goods. More profoundly, this view of rationality denies that meaningful questions can be in principle unanswerable; to allow that they can be is to admit a radical limitation on reason. To admit that genuine questions may not have a single right answer is to impeach a traditional conception of truth, according to which all truths are not merely compatible but in some sense mutually supportive. This is to say that, on this traditional view, not only does every genuine question have one right answer, but that all these answers are mutually compatible, or even entailed by one another. It seems to be this truly fantastic conception of reason that is embedded in the Platonic and Socratic, and even the pre-Socratic, foundations of the Western tradition.[3]

Nor is this foundational view confined to the (Socratic) Greek roots of the Western tradition. It is a feature of the Christian tradition that, however tragic may be the moral and practical dilemmas we face in mortal life, they are all in principle soluble by reference to the will of God; and the ideas of deity and of perfection are conjoined. There cannot, in the Christian view at least, be an ultimate moral tragedy, an unredeemed loss of value or a conflict of right with right, since to allow this would be to subvert the providential order and so undermine the very possibility of theodicy. For a Christian, as perhaps for some Jews and all Muslims, the idea of the best of all possible worlds must be a meaningful one, since, if it is not, the monotheistic conception of divinity is destroyed. These Greek and Christian conceptions came together, in medieval and early modern times, in the doctrine of natural law, which affirmed that the true demands of morality could not issue in irresolvable conflicts.

Berlin rejects this foundational Western commitment. He denies that genuine goods, or authentic virtues, are, necessarily, or as a matter of fact, such that peaceful coexistence among them is a possible state of human life. It is true of many goods, according to Berlin, that they are rivalrous and conflictual. More, Berlin denies that, when such competition among goods occurs, it is always capable of resolution by the application of a rational standard. Human goods are not only often uncombinable; they are sometimes incommensurable. This is Berlin's celebrated doctrine of *value-pluralism*. It has applications at three levels.

First, Berlin affirms that, within any morality or code of conduct such as ours, there will arise conflicts among the ultimate values of that morality, which neither theoretical nor practical reasoning about them can resolve. Within our own liberal morality, for example, liberty and equality, fairness and welfare are recognized as intrinsic goods. Berlin maintains that these goods often collide in practice, that they are inherently rivalrous by nature, and that their conflicts cannot be arbitrated by any overarching standard.

Secondly, *each* of these goods or values is internally complex and inherently pluralistic, containing conflicting elements, some of which are constitutive incommensurables. We have seen already how on Berlin's view liberty, even negative liberty, contains rivalrous and incommensurable liberties: examples may be the liberties of information and of privacy, which are often competitive and which may embody incommensurable values. The same is true of equality, which breaks down on analysis into rival equalities, such as equality of opportunity and equality of outcome. Such goods are not harmonious wholes but themselves arenas of conflict and incommensurability.

Thirdly, different cultural forms will generate different moralities and values, containing many overlapping features, no doubt, but also specifying different, and incommensurable, excellences, virtues and conceptions of the good. Or, to state this third aspect or implication of value-pluralism in another way: There are goods that have as their matrices social structures that are uncombinable; these goods, when they are incommensurables, are also constitutively uncombinable. This is the sort of incommensurability that applies to goods that are constitutive ingredients in whole ways or styles of life. This is the form of incomparability among values, *cultural pluralism*, that is most easily confused with moral relativism – the view that human values are always internal to particular cultural traditions and cannot be the objects of any sort of rational assessment or criticism. Berlin's value-pluralism embraces all three forms or levels of conflict in ethics in that he affirms that incommensurability breaks out in each of them.

It is true of any morality of any complexity and development that it will be riddled with gaps and lacunae, such that it is bound to leave us in the lurch in many a practical dilemma. Similarly, the virtues recognized in any morality will often be unrealizable together in a single individual. Justice and mercy, temperance and courage, may not be fully realizable together in any one individual since they evoke different moral capacities, which cannot easily coexist. There is here a thesis of *moral scarcity* as applied to the virtues which, if it is true, is true as a matter of moral psychology or philosophical anthropology. (In its applications to values other than those of morality – assuming that the distinction between moral and non-moral values can be made and is worth making – value-pluralism of the sort Berlin espouses may be a thesis of abundance, not scarcity. It will be such, in so far as it holds that there is a vast diversity of valuable options, for example, which are uncombinable and among which choices must be made, but which are also incommensurable, so that when one array is chosen in preference to another there is no sense in saying that any definite measure or amount of value has been lost. This non-tragic uncombinability and incommensurability of valuable options is clearly different from conflicts among obligations that cannot be jointly discharged and whose weights are incommensurable.) The deeper content of Berlin's value-pluralism is in the thesis that any complex morality recognizes goods that are in their very natures uncombinable – the goods of autonomous agency and of unreflective decency, perhaps – such that there is a conceptual or logical incoherence in the very idea that a single person at the same time could possess or exercise both. This aspect of Berlin's value-pluralism affirms that any morality which, like our own, is at all complex and developed, will generate for its practitioners moral dilemmas, and rivalries among the virtues, that reasoning cannot resolve. Or, to put the same point in other terms, the perfections identified by any morality such as ours, or by any similar morality, are plural and competitive, and the idea of a perfection that encompasses them all without loss is incoherent.

Pluralism applies also, as we have seen, at the level of whole cultures or traditions, and their associated conceptions of the good. Different forms of life may be animated by distinct moralities which specify discrepant virtues, or which, even if they recognize the same or similar virtues, rank them very differently. The Renaissance morality epitomized in Machiavelli, which expressed a revival of the pagan virtues of the classical world, and to which I will shortly return, contained conceptions of *virtu* and *superbia* which, like the idea of the great-souled man in Aristotle's *Ethics*, are wholly distinct from, and incompatible with, Christian conceptions of humility and brotherly love. Even in the classical world, the virtues that animate the Homeric epic poems are very different from, and incompatible with, those that figure in the Socratic dialogues. These distinct moralities pick out as virtues very different dispositions or traits of character, which will be elements in very different forms of life. Nor is there any overarching or undergirding standard whereby the goods and virtues recognized in different cultural traditions can be put in the balance and weighed. The virtues of the Homeric epics and of the Sermon on the Mount are irreducibly divergent and conflicting, and they express radically different forms of life. There is no Archimedean point of leverage from which they can be judged.

The diversity in ethics Berlin invokes here is what I have called cultural pluralism, the diversity that arises from differences between entire ways of life, as distinct from the differences and conflicts that may arise within any form of life, or within any morality that is at all complex. Such conflicts arising within particular moralities may appear in both of the two forms distinguished earlier – conflicts between goods or values and conflicts within these goods and values. It is worth noting that all three forms of pluralism are found in historical contexts, such as our own, in which cultural traditions are not fully individuated and interpenetrate with one another, and which have a plural inheritance of complex moralities. Indeed, in our own society, which harbours a diversity of highly complex and pluralistic moralities, whose conflicts are often waged within individual lives, the three levels or species of value-pluralism that are marked in Berlin's account are sometimes not at all easy to distinguish from one another.

At this point it may reasonably be asked: What is the status of Berlin's value-pluralism? Is it a position in ethical (or meta-ethical) theory and, if so, how can it be supported? How, in any case, does it differ from the many varieties of scepticism, subjectivism and relativism that are to be found in the history of moral philosophy, and which have been so prevalent in the twentieth century? How are we to understand the central idea of incommensurability, as Berlin deploys it in his argument against the dominant tradition of Western thought? It is clear that these questions demand a persuasive answer, if – as I believe – Berlin's position is a distinctive and novel one that subverts the received orthodoxies in moral and political philosophy, ancient as well as modern. It is, in fact, demonstrable that Berlin's ethical theory is a species, not of relativism or scepticism, but of *objective pluralism*, and that the objective pluralist idea of value-incommensurability is central in giving content to what I have called his agonistic liberalism. The question of whether objective pluralism in ethics *entails* or *supports* agonistic liberalism is one I shall explore in the final chapter of this book. It is worth noting that versions of value-pluralism can be stated, at once less radical and less interesting than Berlin's, which accept that the goods of human life are many, that they are often uncombinable and sometimes constitutively so, but which deny their rational incomparability. In other words, it is possible as a matter of logic to deny monism – the idea that there is a single master-value, together with the related idea that all values are somehow necessarily compatible or harmonious – and yet to insist that all the diversity of goods can be subject to rational judgement as to their weights and rankings. This weaker doctrine of value-pluralism neither presupposes nor entails the thesis that some values are rationally incomparable. It is the stronger version of value-pluralism, in which it is joined to the idea of incommensurability among values, that is Berlin's, however; and I am not persuaded that the weaker version, in which the idea of incommensurability is suppressed, can be stated in any form that does justice to the conflicts of goods we encounter in our actual experience, or which gives substance to the idea of rational choice among goods that have little or nothing in common. At this stage, accordingly, it is reasonable to try to gain a stronger grip on the very idea of incommensurability among values as we find it in Berlin.

Berlin himself finds a powerful, if largely tacit, statement of the thesis of value-pluralism in Machiavelli, of whom he writes:

> If Machiavelli is right, if it is in principle (or in fact: the frontier seems dim) impossible to be morally good and do one's duty as this was conceived by common European, and especially Christian ethics, and at the same time build Sparta or Periclean Athens or the Rome of the Republic or even of the Antonines, then a conclusion of

the first consequence follows: that the belief that the correct, objectively valid solution to the question of how men should live can in principle be discovered, is itself in principle not true ... The idea of the world and of human society as a single intelligible structure is at the root of all the many various versions of natural law – the mathematical harmonies of the Pythagoreans, the logical ladder of Platonic Forms, the genetic-logical pattern of Aristotle, the divine *Logos* of the Stoics and the Christian Churches and of their secularized offshoots. The advance of the natural sciences generated more empirically conceived versions of this image as well as anthropomorphic similes: of Dame Nature as an adjuster of conflicting tendencies (as in Hume or Adam Smith), of Mistress Nature as the teacher of the best way to happiness (as in the works of some French Encyclopedists) ... This unifying monistic pattern is at the very heart of traditional rationalism, religious and atheistic, metaphysical and scientific, transcendental and naturalistic, that has been characteristic of Western civilization. It is this rock, upon which Western beliefs and lives had been founded, that Machiavelli seems, in effect, to have split open. So great a reversal cannot, of course, be due to the acts of a single individual. It could scarcely have taken place in a stable social and moral order; many beside him, medieval nominalists and secularists, Renaissance humanists, doubtless supplied their share of the dynamite ... it was Machiavelli who lit the fatal fuse.[4]

This passage is important, firstly, in identifying Machiavelli as the modern progenitor of the idea that there may be, and indeed are, uncombinable and incommensurable values, virtues, moralities. It is important, secondly, because this idea did not in Machiavelli support liberal conceptions of toleration or diversity – ideals to which, if he had known of them, Machiavelli's attitude would likely have been hostile (as Berlin notes).[5] Value-pluralism of the sort found in

Machiavelli may, as Berlin argues,[6] tend to support liberal ideals of toleration, since it affirms that there is no one right way of life for men; but it did not do so in Machiavelli, and the two conceptions – of value-pluralism and liberal toleration – seem to be logically independent of one another, a point Berlin has himself noted and stressed.[7] The idea of value-pluralism may seem an elusive one for several good reasons.[8] It is not obvious what 'values' designates – goods, options, virtues, whole conceptions of the good or entire cultural traditions or forms of life, or merely wants and preferences. It is the idea of incommensurability itself, however, that seems most elusive to many people. What is it to say that goods are incommensurables? And how might such a claim be supported? What (in other words) is the moral epistemology that underlies objective pluralism in ethics? Is it, as I shall maintain, a variant of *realism* in ethics that is presupposed by the idea of incommensurability about values, such that the claim that there are such values is not an expression of ethical scepticism, but a claim to definite moral knowledge? If Berlin's value-pluralism is, or presupposes, a form of ethical realism that affirms the objectivity of values, how is this to be squared with his insistence that among incommensurables which conflict there cannot be knowledge of the right, but only a groundless decision as to how to act? And what is it in the idea of incommensurability that is so subversive of commonly accepted conceptions of rationality, such that Berlin's claim to have departed from the mainstream of Western philosophy could be justified? What, in short, are the *consequences* of incommensurability for moral and political thought, supposing it to be indeed the truth of the matter? The most illuminating and systematic elucidation of the very idea of value-incommensurability, and one that in most respects accords well with the account of it given by Berlin, is found in the writings of Joseph Raz. We may begin with Raz's observation that to say of two values that they are incommensurable is to say that they cannot be the subject of comparison.[9] Raz's account of incommensurability as incomparability may help us in illuminating the uses Berlin makes of the idea in his ethical and political theory. It is significant that, in Raz's account of it (as, implicitly, in Berlin's), incommensurability of values (goods, options, and so forth) is distinguished sharply from rough equality, and also from indeterminacy. Incommensurability is not rough equality because 'if two options are incommensurate then reason has no judgement to make concerning their relative value. Saying that they are of equal value is passing a judgement about their relative value, whereas saying they are incommensurate is not.'[10] Indeterminacy of value arises when it is neither true nor false that one option is better than another or that they have equal value.[11] Such indeterminacy is a pervasive feature of language and of human action, but it does not seem to capture what is meant by incommensurability. Indeed those who are suspicious or sceptical of the very idea of incommensurability often invoke indeterminacies in our judgements as an alternative to any deeper or more radical denial of commensurability. Incommensurability is thereby eliminated, to be replaced by incompleteness or imperfection in our judgements of value (whether or not such indeterminacy is considered remediable). It is evident that such indeterminacy captures the idea of incommensurability no better than does rough equality of value.

Incommensurability among values discloses itself, instead, as a breakdown or failure in transitivity. 'Two valuable options are incommensurable if 1) neither is better than the other, and 2) there is (or could be) another option which is better than one but is not better than the other.'[12] The *mark of incommensurability* among options or values (as Raz terms it)[13] shows itself when 'If it is possible for one of them to be improved without thereby becoming better than the other, and if there can be another option which is better than the one, but not better than the other, then the two original options are incommensurate.' Examples from outside ethics may give intuitive force to these formal explications. Aeschylus and Shakespeare are each great tragic dramatists, but their dramatic art is incommensurable: it is false to say that the one is a greater dramatist than the other. Nevertheless, it may well be true that Euripides is a greater tragic dramatist than Aeschylus, without it following that Euripides is a greater dramatist than Shakespeare. The original pair of dramatists are incommensurable, because, though their work falls within a single recognizable genre, yet its content and structure, its styles and themes, the background of beliefs and conventions it presupposes, and the forms of life it depicts, are too different for them to be comparable in terms of value as exemplars of tragic drama. This does not prevent us from judging either dramatist's work to be superior to that of a host of his inferior contemporaries', nor – perhaps more interestingly – from judging both to be superior to most drama at all times. (It must not from this, however, be supposed that incommensurability arises only among the best exemplars of a genre. It arises at any level where comparability and thereby transitivity break down.) Or consider examples from architecture. We can recognize great cathedrals that are Gothic or Baroque in style, but, because these styles are so different and have so little in common, we cannot rank a great Gothic cathedral against a great Baroque church. Still less can we rank either against the Taj Mahal or the Zen rock garden at Ryoanji. It is being assumed here, what is plainly not always the case, that there are sufficient continuities within cultures, and overlappings and family resemblances among cultures, for us to be able confidently to individuate particular cultural artefacts as belonging to the same genre. Nothing in the argument for incommensurability rests or turns on this assumption, so far as I can see, since the argument affirms that incommensurabilities of value arise *even when* cross-cultural categorization of artefacts as belonging to the same genres can be reliably made.

Note again that incommensurability is not an incompleteness or an imperfection – in the criteria of value of an object or options, say. It does not arise because criteria of value are multiple and their rankings indeterminate, nor because the boundaries between different categories of objects or options are vague or shifting. There is incommensurability when all of these forms of incompleteness have been removed. As Raz puts it, 'where there is incommensurability, it is the ultimate truth. There is nothing further behind it, nor is it a sign of imperfection.'[14] Nor does incommensurability denote indifference: as Raz puts it incisively, 'Incomparability does not ensure equality of merit and demerit. It does not mean indifference. It marks the inability of reason to guide our action, not the insignificance of our choice.'[15] We are surest that we have identified an incommensurability precisely when none of these indeterminacies are present. In a later statement, Raz clarifies the radical import of value-pluralism in undermining the possibility of comparison between very different ways of life and the goods associated with them:

On a reductive-monistic view (of values) when one trades the pleasures (and anxieties) of a family life for a career as a sailor one is getting, or hoping to get, the same thing one is giving up, be it happiness, pleasure, desire-satisfaction, or something else. So long as one plans correctly and succeeds in carrying out one's plans there is no loss of any kind. One gives up the lesser pleasure one would derive from family life for the greater pleasure of life at sea. If value-pluralism is correct this view is totally wrong. What one loses is of a different kind from what one gains. Even in success there is a loss, and quite commonly there is no meaning to the judgement that one gains more than one loses. When one was faced with valuable options and successfully chose one of them one simply chose one way of life rather than another, both being good and not susceptible to comparison of degree.[16]

By incommensurability, then, is meant incomparability – the incomparability of valuable cultural objects, activities, reasons for action or forms of life. In ethics an implication of incommensurability is the reality of an ultimate diversity of incomparable forms of human excellence or flourishing (and of an equal diversity of incomparable evils). The forms of life of a professional soldier or a spy, of a Buddhist monk, of a courtesan or a gambler who lives by his wits, are not lesser, nor greater, forms of human flourishing than that of the research scientist, the devoted teacher, or the carer in the leprosarium. Contrary to Aristotle, no hierarchy can be established by any rational procedure among such diverse forms of human flourishing. To think otherwise is to invoke an archaic metaphysical biology, itself grounded in an atavistic cosmology of natural ends or a great chain of being, such as is found in Aristotle himself and in Aquinas. This is not to say that there are not poor forms of life, cultural as well as individual, which exhibit few excellences, if any, and which are not recognizably any sort of flourishing. It is only to deny that human flourishing comes in one form, or even a small family of forms.

Value-pluralism bites, as a position in ethical theory, when it is further maintained that such diverse forms of human flourishing are not only rationally incomparable, but also uncombinable, and sometimes constitutively or necessarily uncombinable. The case of the goods of autonomy and of unreflective decency given earlier is an example of a constitutive uncombinability. Uncombinability and incommensurability are, of course, wholly distinct phenomena; uncombinable goods may well be commensurable. The pleasure of a drug-induced ecstasy may be uncombinable with the pleasures of a long life, but – at least on some accounts, such as that given in Bentham's felicific calculus of pleasures and pains – they may be fully commensurable. Furthermore their uncombinability may be more or less radical. It may be that more of one good entails less of another, and in that case, it is the place of practical wisdom to concern itself with good mixtures of such uncombinable, but commensurable, goods. Or it may be that uncombinable goods are alternatives: we can have some of one only at the price of having none of the other. Here, too, the goods concerned may yet be fully commensurable. The rub comes when the goods are constitutively uncombinable, and *also* incommensurable. This is often the case when the goods concerned are bound up with wholly distinct and incompatible forms of social life; but it can occur also within cultural traditions which acknowledge distinct vocations, each with their associated virtues. Such cultural traditions are normal in human history. As Hampshire has noted:

> So great has been the influence within contemporary moral philosophy of Hume, Kant and the Utilitarians that it has been possible to forget that for centuries the warrior and the priest, the landowner and the peasant, the merchant and the craftsman, the musician or poet who lives by his performances, have coexisted in society with sharply distinct dispositions and virtues . . . Varied social roles and functions, each with its typical virtues and its peculiar obligations, have been the normal situation in most societies throughout history.[17]

Within any complex culture, there will typically be a diversity of forms of life, each with its associated virtues and excellences, available to many people, but it will not be possible to combine these forms of life within the compass of a single biography. This may be because the virtues of a nun, say, constitutively exclude those of a lover, or it may be because, though different virtues can be combined in a single person, they tend to crowd one another out, or to be conjointly realizable only at the cost of each being achieved at a low level. We have here examples of the moral scarcity alluded to earlier. Forms of human flourishing may be constitutively uncombinable because they belong with, or presuppose as their matrices, social structures, or entire cultural traditions, that are themselves constitutively uncombinable. Or else they may be uncombinable at this deep constitutive level because they demand in the individual agent virtues or excellences that cannot, as a matter of moral psychology or philosophical anthropology, be realized together. This latter species of value-conflict may be called empirical inasmuch as it depends on features of ourselves and our circumstances that could conceivably be otherwise – however difficult it may be to envisage such a contingency. The deeper conflict of goods or virtues that occurs between constitutively uncombinable incommensurables may be termed (as it often is by Berlin) conceptual rather than empirical.

It may be that there is a connection between the conceptual impossibility of combining radically different cultural forms and the incommensurabilities in meaning explored in recent philosophy of science, but, if so, it is not a connection that Berlin's account emphasizes. Indeed he is at pains to insist that, even between widely divergent forms of cultural life, there can be mutual understanding and communication, of the sort that relativism, and so theses of meaning-incommensurability, deny or foreclose upon. Further, the conceptual impossibility of combining some virtues may, for Berlin, arise even within a single form of cultural life, with a common (if complex) vocabulary, which precludes semantic incommensurability. It seems that Berlin's claim is that the very nature of central human powers is such that they and their attendant goods are inherently competitive with each other, and not, as Aristotle complacently supposed, mutually supportive.

Nor is this competition restricted in its scope to moral life. It will often be the case of goods in individual lives that are not moral goods and of excellences that are not virtues. (I leave aside here the large and important issue, explored profoundly in Bernard Williams' work,[18] of whether our present conception of morality as a distinct sphere of practical life and deliberation has any claim on reason, and the related question, whether the distinctions we make between moral and non- moral reasons, and between mere excellences and moral virtues, are non-arbitrary, defensible, or even fully intelligible.) So it may be that intellectual powers of rigorous analysis cannot be fully developed in coexistence, in the same person, with great powers of imaginative empathy. Or, as noted in the preceding chapter, it may be that the creative power of a great artist wanes as the artist's self-knowledge waxes. If this is so – as seems plainly sometimes to be the case – then it will not be in virtue of the shortness of human lives, or any other scarcity of resources, but because the goods and virtues concerned are competitive in their very natures. Where this is not a question of their depending for their realization on social structures that cannot be mixed, it is true as a matter of moral psychology. That this facet of value-pluralism is in Berlin an anthropological thesis – at least in part – is a point to which I shall return later in this chapter.

Berlin's pluralist thesis of the incomparability of ultimate or fundamental values applies to evils as well as to goods. Though this is less often stressed in his account, it is affirmed in his insistence on the reality of moral tragedy, which moral philosophy as a discipline seems bent on exorcizing from conscious awareness. Here too it reveals itself as a breakdown in transitivity.[19] I may judge that a totalitarian regime in which human freedom is pervasively repressed, but in which there is little, if any, political murder is more, or less, of an evil, than a traditional tyranny that is far less repressive of freedom, but in which political murder is a commonplace. The point is that, whatever my judgement may be, it will not be transmissible transitively, if what we have are truly incommensurables, to a third regime, having different features, even if we can rank this third regime against *either* of the original pair. The reason lies in the incommensurability of the repression of individual freedom with political violence. The Czechoslovak regime of the 1970s, which was a totalitarian regime sustained principally by economic coercion rather than by political violence, is plausibly incommensurable with the Nicaraguan Somoza regime, which was a murderous traditional tyranny. We might judge a third regime – the communist regime in Mongolia, say – to be worse than either of the previous two, because it contained both the incommensurable evils of political violence and pervasive economic coercion; if so, we have a case where two regimes that may not be rationally comparable as to their badness are commensurable with a third that is worse than either. Or we may judge yet another regime – that of communist Yugoslavia, for example – to be worse than the Nicaraguan regime, without judging it to be worse than the Czechoslovak regime; in this case, we see clearly the difference between incommensurability and rough equality. This breakdown in comparability among the evils of human life is important if, as Berlin sometimes indicates, it is a feature of his pluralism that it not only denies the combinability of all goods, but also affirms the dependency of many goods upon evils. This will be true, in Berlin's view and in mine, on any view of good and evil that is realistic and faithful to experience: it will be true, and perhaps most clearly true, when the evils and goods are identified naturalistically, without the use of any theistic or metaphysical premises. What is worthy of note is that incommensurabilities arising from conflicts of goods with evils, which are the lifeblood of fiction and drama, should be such strangers in moral philosophy, when they are recognized in that subject at all.

Berlin's value-pluralism has been discerned, by Berlin himself, in such writers as Machiavelli, Montesquieu, Vico, and Herder, if not as an explicit doctrine, then as an unarticulated presupposition of their thought. The question arises whether the doctrine itself is original, as we find it in Berlin's works. That, in moral life, we must trade off values without the help that might be given us by any overarching principle, was the view of the moral intuitionists, such as Ross and Rashdall, whose works were read in Oxford in the

Twenties, when Berlin was a student there; but there is not in Berlin any intuitionist conception of a moral sense whereby conflicts among incommensurable values are somehow reconciled, nor is there, in the intuitionists, any insight into the incommensurability of the goods associated with whole forms of life. It may safely be conjectured that Berlin's value-pluralism owes little, if anything, to the Oxford intuitionists. A more plausible affinity may be found in the work of Max Weber, quoted by Berlin,[20] when Weber invokes clashes of irreconcilable values, and indeed of irreconcilable moralities, in political life. What is lacking in Weber is any account of the sources of such clashes in moral psychology, in philosophical anthropology, or in conflict between different cultural forms. Nevertheless, if there is an explicit anticipation of Berlinian value-pluralism to be found anywhere, it is in Weber's thought, where it supports an agonistic view of political life that has many points of contact with Berlin's.

It is worth considering further the implications of Berlinian pluralism for ethical theory and, thereby, for political thought. Perhaps the most straightforward implication is the death-blow it deals, if it is true, to utilitarianism. For utilitarian or consequentialist ethics in all their forms depend on the possibility of aggregation among utilities and of summation among consequences, or in general, on comparability among the states of affairs that enter into utilitarian assessment, and this the thesis of incommensurability destroys. Bentham's felicific calculus, if value-pluralism is true, is an attempt to perform the impossible, to weigh and rank irreducibly diverse and incomparable goods in a single scale. The pluralist thesis is that the goods of human life are in many instances not scalar or additive. This undermines the possibility of such comparative judgements of global utility as are involved in contemporary preference utilitarianism as well as in the classical, mental-state versions of utilitarianism. Note that nothing in pluralism hinges on difficulties in making *interpersonal* comparisons of utility: pluralism subverts the possibility, in many cases, of such judgements *within individual lives*. Note also that Berlin's pluralism is not the claim that there are occasional pockets of incommensurability, such that utilitarian maximization is not always a possibility: it is the more radical claim – but also the more defensible claim, if human experience is to be our guide – that incommensurability is pretty pervasive in human life and so in practical reasoning. The objection to utilitarianism is not merely that incommensurability circumscribes the possibilities of maximization on which utilitarianism depends; it is that the utilitarian vision of the best state of affairs is very often a mirage. If Berlin is right, we have in general no coherent conception of what the best state of affairs would be like. Always acting for the best is an illegitimate strategy in moral life, not because it comes up against deontic (justice-based) constraints of duty or right, but because it is often true that we *cannot* (and not simply do not) know what is the best state of affairs, even when all relevant imperfections and indeterminacies in our knowledge and judgement have been allowed for.

Berlin's pluralism distinguishes his liberalism starkly from that of John Stuart Mill. To be sure, Millian liberalism is tender towards human diversity. It was one of Mill's chief contentions that the demands of happiness or flourishing differ in individual cases, perhaps because individuals have natures, or quiddities, containing endowments and needs that are in many respects unique or peculiar to them. A liberal society is commended because, via 'experiments in living', it will shelter many varieties of individual flourishings. There may indeed be tensions in Mill's thought, between his conviction of the diversity of human nature, and of the individuality of the forms of flourishing that are appropriate for each person, and his account of the higher pleasures, conceived as a determinate set of activities or satisfactions involving the exercise of the distinctively human powers and capacities. It is taken for granted by Mill that the higher pleasures will be moral and intellectual in character, rather than bodily and sensuous, say. It does not occur to him that, if human nature contains the diversity and individuality he claims for it, then different people will elect to develop different generically human powers and capabilities. Nor does he perceive that the development of some of these powers may hinder that of others. It does not occur to him, for example, that the development of the pleasures of the palate, or of sexual pleasure, may make demands on the definitively human powers as great as the development of the analytical capacities or of imaginative sympathy, such as are involved in the pursuit of philosophy or enjoyment of the arts, so that one kind of higher pleasure will tend to drive others out. Most radically, he does not confront the fact that, within the range of the higher pleasures, even of those that are accessible to any one individual and which are appropriate to that individual in virtue of his nature, there will be uncombinabilities, some of which will be constitutive rather than contingent. Thus, an individual may contain within himself needs for both risk-taking and for security, for novelty and for the happiness that comes from repetition, and satisfying these needs may involve the development of capacities, dispositions, excellences and virtues that cannot coexist. (I leave aside here the interesting issues suggested by people whose lives correspond to Parfit's idea of earlier and later selves,[21] since to explore them properly would lead us too far afield.) In short, Mill does not confront the realities of conflict and even of contradiction within individual natures, facts which qualify, if they do not altogether destroy, the ideal of rounded or harmonious individuality which he absorbed from Humboldt. It is precisely the radical choices demanded by the complexity and conflicting needs of individual natures that are addressed by Berlin.

Mill's liberalism diverges from Berlin's, also, of course, in that it is supposed by Mill to have a utilitarian foundation. I have myself argued that Mill's claim that a liberal society as the best for happiness is, at best, a not unreasonable wager, which the available evidence does not decisively contradict.[22] A deeper objection, made by Berlin,[23] is that the idea of happiness has in Mill so mutated that its use in any sort of felicific calculus is not a possibility: it has come to designate precisely that irreducible diversity of human goods which Berlin's pluralism identifies. This is to say that, contrary to all of his intentions, Mill's liberalism is not, in the end, an application of utilitarian ethics, for liberal utilitarianism is not ultimately a viable position in moral and political thought. In the end, Mill values choice and individuality for their own sakes, not because they best promote general happiness. If this be admitted, Mill's and Berlin's liberalisms are brought closer together, but they are still far apart. For a central aspect of Mill's project, as much in *The System of Logic* and *Utilitarianism* as in *On Liberty*, is the development of a theory which will govern practical life. There cannot, for Mill, be undecidable dilemmas in moral or political life, since that would impeach the ideal of rationality central to classical utilitarianism, and from which, despite his many other revisions of his utilitarian inheritance, he never departed. Millian liberalism accordingly precludes the idea of radical choice – choice without criteria, grounds, or principles – that is the heart of Berlin's liberalism.

We reach at this point one of the most distinctive and important implications of Berlin's pluralism for political thought. It diverges, not only from utilitarianism but also from Kantian ethics and from Lockean theories of fundamental rights, in denying that a coherent political morality can be formulated that is expressed in a single principle or an ordered system of principles. The idea that there is a structure of compossible rights,[24] or a system of dovetailing side-constraints,[25] or a set of basic liberties,[26] as these ideas are developed in other recent liberal thinkers in a Kantian tradition, such as Steiner, Nozick, and Rawls, is rejected by Berlin. Utility may collide and conflict with liberty, liberty with equality, individuality with community: none of these values or political goods is derivative from any other, each is an ultimate end and intrinsic value, and their conflicts cannot be resolved by appeal to any synoptic moral theory. Contrary to Dworkin, who maintains[27] that it is an idea of equality that is foundational in liberalism, Berlin is clear that it is freedom that is the central liberal value. He is no less clear that the claims of freedom are never absolutist, that it is reasonable, and for that matter unavoidable, to trade off liberty for other values, and to engage in trade-offs among conflicting liberties, including negative liberties, where these are sometimes incommensurables. Accordingly, though he affirms that freedom is the constitutive value of liberal political morality, he denies that there can be a theory of the fundamental right to liberty. Most importantly, he is insistent that the task of philosophy is to illuminate such conflicts, not to prescribe the trade-offs that we make. For Berlin, no theory or principle can govern these choices, precisely because they are radical choices among incommensurables.

Here the critic may ask: If there can be no theory whereby such choices are moderated, how does Berlin's pluralism differ in the end from moral scepticism or relativism? What distinguishes it from the plethora of subjectivist doctrines that have dominated twentieth-century ethics? The vital difference is in Berlin's claim that we *know* that the conflicts between ultimate values are genuine: that they are conflicts among goods that are irreducible and incommensurable. We have knowledge of moral reality, such that to affirm otherwise is to falsify it. Here Berlin's argument is akin to that he advances against determinism. It is a fundamental feature of our ordinary experience that goods conflict, just as it is that we are free subjects, not deterministic objects. Only an overwhelmingly powerful theory could hope to displace these phenomenological certainties; and this we lack, in both cases. Berlin's variant of ethical realism asserts a moral reality that is underdetermined, in that although its contents are highly determinate, as are their conflicts, there is no 'right answer' when these conflicts are among incommensurables. Further, our experience is that such conflicts are sometimes tragic, in that whatever we do, we commit a wrong, on occasion an irreparable one. Why should we seek to displace this datum of experience at the behest of any ethical theory? It is not as if such theories were themselves especially compelling. Berlin's pluralism is not a sceptical view, then, because he affirms such radical value-conflict as a matter of moral knowledge, the denial of which is (as Williams has well put it) a departure from truthfulness,[28] from fidelity to our actual experience.

It is *not* denied, by Berlin or by any other exponent of incommensurability, that our experience could be so impoverished that many occasions for choice among incommensurables would no longer arise. Indeed, if utilitarian, Kantian, or any other species of moral rationalism were adopted, it might well destroy many of the goods that generate such incommensurabilities. There is nothing incoherent in a rationalist moral theory seeking to render commensurable goods that, in our experience of moral life, are not commensurable. In part this is a possibility because many incommensurable goods are dependent for their existence on specific practices, or cultural forms, which a rationalist reconstitution of moral life would undermine or destroy. In our society, the good of friendship is not commensurable with that of money: we do not charge a consultation fee for listening to our friends' troubles and, if we did, that would signify the death of friendship as a practice among us. There is, in all probability, nothing to prevent such a transformation in our moral life since, though the good of friendship is at least as old as Aristotle, it may not be a universally or generically human good. This shows (as Raz perceives)[29] that incommensurabilities, even among constitutively uncombinable goods, may be shattered by changes in their constitutive conventions. A utilitarian, say, who proposes that very painful medical experimentation on a child be put in a

felicific calculus and rendered commensurable with the
production of better aspirins, cannot be convicted of any
inconsistency in reasoning, but only of insensitivity to the
forms of moral life from which arises the incommensurability of such experimentation with the relief of mild pain.
A Kantian theorist who will not commit an injustice to
prevent a worse evil, where these are commensurable, or
who denies that there are undecidable moral dilemmas in
which whatever is chosen entails wrong, cannot be given
demonstrative arguments which compel the abandonment
of his moral theory. The question is rather which should be
accorded primacy – the phenomenological realities of moral
life, or the demands of theory. For Berlin, the phenomenology of moral life, which abounds in incommensurabilities
and radical choices, merits primacy, if only because of the
striking feebleness of the moral theories which seek to displace it. The fact is that we do not have a workable felicific
calculus, or an account of a structure of compossible rights.
We have no reason to abandon the richness and depth of
moral life, with all of its undecidable dilemmas, for the
empty vistas of moral theory.

With respect to those goods that are specific to definite
forms of life, and are not universal, then, incommensurability can be overcome by a destruction of the constitutive
conventions that generate the goods. Such is the project, it
seems, of utilitarianism and Kantian ethics. According to
Berlin, however, there are universal, or near-universal, categories of moral thought, which are not vulnerable to
theoretical displacement, and which also generate incommensurabilities. There are, also, universal goods of fairness
and well-being, universal virtues of courage and sympathy,
that are generically human, and which generate the 'minimum content of natural law' to which H. L. A. Hart
famously refers.[30] Berlin's thesis is that conflicts within this
core of universal values are themselves universal and
endemic. His account of this universal matrix of generically
human categories of moral thought distinguishes his view

from any sort of relativism, but also, in virtue of the incommensurabilities and undecidable dilemmas it contains, from any natural law tradition. It is his view that the universal content of morality itself generates irresolvable conflicts among its constitutive values that is most distinctive and original, rather than any account he gives of the particular elements of this universal content.

His view as to the latter is clearly that it is an anthropological matter. It is not wholly clear how the universal content of morality is to be known; as we shall see, for Berlin, specifying its content cannot be an entirely or straightforwardly empirical affair. Nonetheless it will doubtless be partly determined by empirical anthropology, which will disclose family resemblances among moralities, in terms of which a universal framework is exemplified. The forms of this exemplification will be highly diverse, as these universal values assume different historical embodiments. However, the conflicts these universal values occasion are, for Berlin, no less a matter of knowledge than the particularities of the values themselves. Once again, his is a realist view: we can *know*, partly by empirical anthropology, what the common framework of human moral thought is, and we can *know* – partly by empirical anthropology, partly by the phenomenology of moral life as we ourselves have experienced it – that it generates undecidable dilemmas. We can know, for example, that the good of romantic love is a local matter, a specific cultural form, such that its incommensurability with other goods can be overcome by the disappearance or mutation of this local practice and its constitutive virtues. But, equally, we can know that nothing short of an alteration in human nature could prevent justice from colliding with mercy, prudence with courage. To acknowledge such collisions is, in Berlin's view, the first desideratum of moral theory. It is a commentary on moral philosophy as a discipline that it has, from its inception, sought to deny, or to dispel, these conflicts.

We return here to the question of the place in Berlin's

thought of a common human nature. It is, I think, only in a common framework of categories of thought, together with the distinctive human capacity for choice-making that itself imports an element of essential indeterminacy in our natures, that Berlin allows the idea of a common human nature at all, aside from the constraints on self-creation imposed by our animal biological inheritance. Even the most basic biological human needs find very diverse expressions in different cultures. More radically, Berlin's view of man as a species whose needs and nature are subject to self-transformation through choice-making, and whose most essential mark is cultural difference, forbids any idea of a common human nature, at least as that is ordinarily understood. We might even say, adapting Wollheim,[31] that for Berlin, there is a common human nature, but that it is exhibited only in the divergent natures human beings constitute for themselves, subject to the constraints of their biological and historical inheritances.

There is nevertheless an ambiguity, or at least an unclarity, in Berlin's account of the universal categories that constitute the common framework of moral thought. Are these 'categories' quasi-Kantian presuppositions of any kind of moral judgement or reasoning, or are they substantive moral norms that are putatively universal? We have here an indeterminacy in Berlin's thought which parallels that afflicting his use of the term 'values'. When Berlin speaks of goods or evils that are generically human, or of virtues that occur in all known forms of moral life, he seems to conceive of the common framework of moral thought as having a *substantive* content that is universal. In this case, there would have to be an enduring or constant core in human nature, a common human nature, from which the universal element in morality springs. On the other hand we find Berlin stressing again and again that man is a self-transforming animal, that nothing in his thought is in principle immune from alteration by the growth of knowledge, that human needs are altered by changes in our conceptions of them and by the unpredictable consequences of human choices, and that many human virtues and excellences are dependent upon, and partly constituted by, cultural forms that are historically specific. Where is the room in this historicist view for a common human nature? We have also a question about our knowledge of these categories. So far we have found Berlin treating them as anthropological generalizations, which are presumably known empirically. At the same time, when he discusses the question of our knowledge of these 'categories' explicitly, we find him denying that they, or our knowledge of them, are straightforwardly empirical, even though he insists that they cannot be insulated from the growth of scientific knowledge.

Accordingly, referring to 'the categories in terms of which we discuss men's ends or duties or interests, the permanent framework in terms of which, not about which, ordinary empirical disagreement can arise', Berlin asks: 'What are these categories? How do we discover them? If not empirically, then by what means? How universal and unchanging are they? How do they enter into and shape the models and paradigms in terms of which we think and respond? Do we discover what they are by attention to thought, or action, or unconscious processes, and how do we reconcile these various sources of knowledge?' He goes on: 'These are characteristically philosophical questions, since they are questions about the all but permanent ways in which we think, decide, perceive, judge, and not about the data of experience – the items themselves. The test of the adequate working of the methods, analogies, models which operate in discovering and classifying the behaviour of these empirical data (as natural science and common sense do) is ultimately empirical: it is the degree of their success in forming a coherent and enduring conceptual system.' Berlin is clear that these categories do not have the a priori status ascribed to them in Kant's philosophy: 'Kant supposed these categories to be discoverable *a priori*. We need not accept this; this was an unwarranted conclusion from the valid perception that there exist central features of our experience that are invariant and omnipresent, or at least much less variable than the vast variety of its empirical characteristics, and for that reason deserve to be distinguished by the name of categories.'[32] Though not a priori in the Kantian sense, these categories are not inductive generalizations either: 'The basic categories (together with their corresponding concepts)' Berlin tells us, 'in terms of which we define men – such notions as society, freedom, sense of time and change, suffering, happiness, productivity, good and bad, right and wrong, choice, effort, truth, illusion (to take them wholly at random) – are not matters of induction or hypothesis. To think of someone as a human being is *ipso facto* to bring all these notions into play: so that to say of someone that he is a man, but that choice, or the notion of truth, mean nothing to him, would be eccentric: it would clash with what we mean by "man" not as a matter of verbal definition (which is alterable at will), but as intrinsic to the way we think, and (as a matter of "brute" fact) evidently cannot but think.' Berlin concludes: 'This will hold of values too (among them political ones) in terms of which men are defined. Thus if I say of someone that he is kind or cruel, loves truth or is indifferent to it, he remains human in either case. But if I find a man to whom it literally makes no difference whether he kicks a pebble or kills his family, since either would be an antidote to *ennui* or inactivity, I shall not be disposed, like consistent relativists, to attribute to him merely a different code of morality from my own or that of most men, but shall begin to speak of insanity and inhumanity; I shall be inclined to consider him mad, as a man who thinks he is Napoleon is mad; which is a way of saying that I do not regard such a being as being fully a man at all. It is cases of this kind, which seem to make it clear that ability to recognize universal – or almost universal – values enters into our analysis of such fundamental concepts as "man", "rational", "sane", "natural", etc. – which are usually thought of as descriptive and not evaluative – that lie at the basis of modern translations into empirical terms of the kernel of truth in the old a priori natural law tradition. It is considerations such as these, urged by neo-Aristotelians and the followers of the later doctrines of Wittgenstein, that have shaken the faith of some devoted empiricists in the complete logical gulf between descriptive statements and statements of value, and have cast doubt on the celebrated distinction derived from Hume.'[33]

These statements suggest that, for Berlin, the common human framework of moral categories is neither a priori in the full Kantian sense nor an empirical generalization of supposedly universal substantive moral norms, but something in between these two things. It is best understood, perhaps, in terms of the later philosophy of Wittgenstein, as a matter of family resemblances among the moral judgements members of different cultures are apt to make. If it is thought of in this way, the 'common core' of human values need not be supposed to be fixed, or wholly determinate in its content. This is to say that, on Berlin's view, it is not possible to state, once and for all, in advance of any changes in our scientific and anthropological knowledge, in the manner of Kant, what are the permanent categories of human thought, including moral thought. Neither is the specification of a 'common framework' of moral categories or a 'common core' of human values – with all the ambiguity between conceptual structures and substantive norms that these expressions contain – a matter of simple historical and anthropological generalization. Rather, by a mode of inquiry that Berlin calls philosophical but to which advances in our empirical knowledge remain always relevant, he claims we can identify a common structure in human thought about moral matters in terms of which moral dilemmas are themselves generated and identified.

There may be an unclarity, or perhaps an unresolved tension, in the conception of philosophic method, and indeed of philosophy itself, which these statements presuppose. Berlin's account of philosophy as the intellectual activity which deals with questions that are neither formal nor empirical, and in which we lack clear or agreed criteria for assessing rival answers to these questions,[34] coheres well with his account of the common structure of moral thought, but it remains unclear how far the results of philosophical inquiry are (on Berlin's account of it) unavoidably time-bound. Here I want only to note that Berlin does not follow Kant in thinking that the structure of human thought, or of moral concepts, is fixed and unalterable. For Berlin, this structure – composed of categories or norms such as fairness, truth, and so on – is highly abstract, and so may be manifested in a great variety of ways, each of which will be historically and culturally specific; and its content can never be specified exhaustively, once for all, as Kant thought it might. When reference is made, later in my exposition of Berlin's thought, to the common core, these ambiguities and indeterminacies in it will be taken for granted. The place in his distinctive version of liberalism of this common element in the moral judgements of mankind will be subject to critical scrutiny in the final chapter.

Berlin's most original claim about this common framework is that its structure is such as to generate dilemmas that are unavoidable and at the same time undecidable by reason. He claims that the categories of thought that undergird the common judgement of mankind generate conflicts that are objective and of which it is true that they have no right solution. The very common framework of thought that assures the objectivity of moral reasoning also shows us that some moral conflicts are insoluble by reason. This is the nub of Berlin's pluralism, and what distinguishes it from every kind of relativism and subjectivism, as well as from all traditional doctrines of natural law.

Berlin's pluralism, in its implications for moral and political thought, may perhaps now be provisionally summarized. Its first implication is a rejection of the idea of a perfect society, or a perfect human life. This rejection is not the banal and shallow repudiation of perfectibilism, advanced on fallibilist grounds by Popper, nor is it the Augustinian affirmation of human imperfectibility that is a cliché of conservative thought; it is the much more radical and original thesis that the very idea of perfection is vacuous or incoherent. As we shall see, the pluralist rejection of the idea of perfection as incoherent is also fatal to the conception of human history as at least potentially progressive, and of similar forms of meliorism, of the sort found in Popper and J. S. Mill and, for that matter, in Hayek and in Burke. Its second implication is that a developed morality – say, liberal political morality – cannot have a hierarchical structure, such that practical dilemmas are decidable by the application of a system of principles. In political life, as in moral life, we are in the business of making trade-offs between conflicting goods and evils, where the weights of these values are given to us by no supreme principle. They are goods without a common currency for their measurement, between which we must nevertheless choose. Such groundless and criterionless choice is the stuff of moral and political life, in so far as it is pervaded by incommensurabilities. Its third implication is that, in such radical dilemmas of choice, reason leaves us in the lurch. When practical and theoretical reason run out, as they must when we are confronted by incommensurables, we have no choice but to act. In this respect the very expression 'radical choice' may be oxymoronic, for in the undecidable dilemmas marked in Berlinian pluralism, our option can only be to act, not to engage in further reflective deliberation, as the language of choice-making suggests. There is in Berlin's idea of radical choice arising from conflicts among incommensurables a decisionist, voluntarist, or existentialist element that distinguishes it from all, or virtually all, forms of liberal rationalism.

The diversity of human natures produced by choice-making of this radical sort is not, of course, only or even primarily, in Berlin's account of it, a diversity of individual natures. Self-creation through choice-making occurs not only in individual life but also collectively. Human beings constitute themselves, not only as individual agents, but as practitioners of diverse cultural traditions, with distinctive collective identities. They form for themselves divergent worlds of practice, distinct forms of discourse and thought, each with its own history. It is these diverse networks of practice, indeed, that, in Berlin's account, as in the later Wittgenstein's, accord to moral judgement its objectivity. Berlin's variant of ethical realism is accordingly what is sometimes termed *internal realism*.[35] On this realist view the elements in the world of value, though they are historical creations – forms of activity, such as science or art, forms of life, such as friendship or romantic love – are nevertheless independent subject-matters, in respect of which our beliefs may be true or false. To this extent Berlin appears to share the later Wittgenstein's notion of objectivity as publicness, as specifying that which belongs to the world of common practices. Whether this commits Berlin to a *pluralist epistemology*, a generalized statement of the plural realism he holds to in ethics, is a question I shall leave to the final chapter of this book.

At this point in the argument it is worth emphasizing that, though the forms of life human beings invent for themselves are immensely diverse, they are not in Berlin's account of them for that reason inaccessible or incommunicable to one another. On the contrary, these practices are, according to Berlin, mutually intelligible to a high degree: they are not the self-enclosed *weltanschauungen* or ideologies of relativism, hermetically sealed off from one another. They have the objectivity that comes from their being public and from their mutual intelligibility. Again, there is nothing subjectivist in Berlin's account of value-pluralism, if only because, though he conceives of individual identities as products of self-creation through choice-making, he perceives that such choice-making occurs always in a context of the inherited choices of earlier generations and the contemporaneous choices of others. Even the creation of an individual identity presupposes the social forms constituted in earlier acts of collective self-creation.[36] Berlin's is not a subjectivist account of value, then, partly because moral practices are conceived as common forms of life possessing the objectivity that comes from their publicity, and also because the agents who make moral choices and judgements are always partly constituted by forms of common life and by historic inheritances of practice. The identities of human agents are always, in Berlin's view of them, embedded in common forms of life, themselves understood as essentially historic creations.

There is in Berlin's thought, however, a deeply voluntarist element, inasmuch as he emphasizes that our common practices generate dilemmas they cannot themselves resolve and which demand decisions for which reasons cannot in the end be given. This voluntarism qualifies Berlin's version of internal realism about values in that it acknowledges that justification of action by reference to common or public practices comes to an end. At the same time, for Berlin – unlike, say, the early Sartre, or Fichte – the role of will in human life is always circumscribed by the common world of human practices. This must be so, if the very identities of agents are always partly inheritances, and products of unchosen participation in common forms of life. We are engaged in self-creation by choice-making, but never *ex nihilo*; for the self that transforms itself through the choices it makes is itself unchosen, since it is always a deposit of the choices made by others, now and in generations that have gone before. Indeed, as we shall see later, Berlin's belief that choice-making is a power of agents whose identities are always partly inheritances, deeply shaped by the language and form of life that is contingently theirs, is bound to qualify his idea of radical choice or wilful decision. Many of the most momentous 'choices' we make may turn out on examination – if this latter belief of Berlin's is at all well-founded – not to express 'decisions' we have made, but to be summations or precipitates of our experiences and of the forms of life to which we belong. We may be part-authors of our lives, then, but these are always variations on common texts.[37]

Never of one text, however, the text of universal humanity as recorded in universal history, as that was understood in the Enlightenment. For it is Berlin's thesis that the self-creation of the human species is always itself plural, never singular, so that the idea of a single human history, the history of the species as such, is as misconceived and incoherent as the idea of a perfect human life, which it is the deepest import of his pluralism to subvert. If there is an essential indeterminacy in human nature, such that the ordinary conception of a common or constant human nature has no useful application, then the idea of a universal human history will be similarly unfounded. It will be true of human history, as some have thought true of language, that it is necessarily manifold: that, just as it is in the nature of language that there be many languages, so there are always many human histories, never only one.[38] The idea of a universal human history is inconsistent with the insight that cultural difference is the expression of man's only partly determinate nature. We may put Berlin's insight into the jargon of post-modernism by saying that it is a consequence of the conception of human beings that he invokes that they should tell a diversity of narratives about themselves, none of which has the authority of a meta-narrative. History will on Berlin's account of it have all the unpredictability, variety and novelty one would expect from a self-transforming species. This is a historicist conception of human nature. It is historicist inasmuch as human identities, the diverse natures formed for itself by an inventive species, are historical creations, webs spun across the generations. This is a historicist, and not a naturalistic conception of human nature akin to that of Hume, say, inasmuch as it conceives of human identities as diverse forms of self-creation and self-transformation of the species and not as mere variations on a constant nature that is held in common by all the species. Indeed we may say that Berlin's historicist conception of human nature is the anthropological premise, or presupposition, of his value-pluralism, inasmuch as it asserts as a primordial propensity of the human species the disposition to form for itself a plurality of diverse natures, or (what comes to the same thing) to invent for itself a variety of forms of life. It is this pluralist aspect of Berlin's philosophical anthropology that distinguishes it from other historicist conceptions, such as Marx's.

That Berlin's is a historicist conception of human nature cannot reasonably be doubted. At the same time, the idea that there are laws of historical development for the species as a whole – *this* doctrine of historicism – will be rejected, even as the idea that the forms of human nature that we find around us are historical creations is endorsed. In his rejection of a scientific history, accordingly, we find in Berlin a commitment to methodological pluralism that parallels, or complements, his deepest idea of value-pluralism. For the central thesis of his methodological pluralism is that the discourses of the different intellectual disciplines are irreducibly diverse. This anti-reductionist view is one that recurs time and again in Berlin's work, and supports his rejection of the positivist ideal of a unified science. The conception of a deterministic science of human history, or of human conduct in general, runs aground on conceptual incoherences, just as the idea of a perfect society, of a form of life containing the whole range of the best achievements of all forms of life, breaks down on conceptual impossibilities. It is to Berlin's view of history that we now turn.

3 History

It would be generally agreed that the reverse of a grasp of
reality is the tendency to fantasy or Utopia. But perhaps
there exist more ways than one to defy reality. May it not
be that to be unscientific is to defy, for no good logical or
empirical reason, established hypotheses and laws; while to
be unhistorical is the opposite – to ignore or twist one's
view of particular events, persons, predicaments, in the
name of laws, theories, principles derived from other fields,
logical, ethical, metaphysical, scientific, which the nature
of the medium renders inapplicable? For what else is it that
is done by those theorists who are called fanatical because
their faith in a given pattern is not overcome by their sense
of reality? For this reason the attempt to construct a
discipline which would stand to concrete history as pure to
applied, no matter how successful the human sciences may
grow to be – even if, as all but obscurantists must hope, they
discover genuine, empirically confirmed, laws of individual
and collective behaviour – seems an attempt to square the
circle. It is not a vain hope for an ideal beyond human
powers, but a chimera, born of lack of understanding of
the nature of natural science, or of history, or of both.

Isaiah Berlin, 'The Concept of Scientific History'[1]

To a disciple of Vico, the ideal of some of the thinkers of
the Enlightenment, the notion of even the abstract
possibility of a perfect society, is necessarily an attempt to
weld together incompatible attributes – characteristics,
ideals, gifts, properties, values that belong to different
patterns of thought, action, life, and therefore cannot be
detached and sewn together in one garment. For a Vichian
this notion must be literally absurd: absurd because there is
a conceptual clash between, let us say, what gives splendour
to Achilles and what causes Socrates or Michelangelo or

Spinoza or Mozart or the Buddha to be admired; and since this applies to the respective cultures, in the context of which alone men's achievements can be understood and judged, this fact alone makes this particular dream of the Enlightenment incoherent. The scepticism or pessimism of a good many thinkers of the Enlightenment – Voltaire, Hume, Gibbon, Grimm, Rousseau – about the possibility of realizing this condition is beside the point. The point is that even they were animated by a conception of clear possibilities, however unattainable in practice. In this, at least, they seem to be at one with the more optimistic Turgot and Condorcet. After Vico, the conflict of monism and pluralism, timeless values and historicism, was bound sooner or later to become a central issue.

Isaiah Berlin, 'Vico and the Ideal of the Enlightenment'[2]

Berlin's view of history is of a piece with his pluralism and his rejection of determinism. It expresses a view of human nature in which cultural forms are exfoliations of the species, unpredictable in their development and often uncombinable with one another, episodes in its self-creation through choice-making, and as irreducibly diverse as are natural human languages. This is his pluralism as applied to history – his insight that cultural difference is coeval with mankind. It is the application to history of his *pluralist anthropology* – his assertion of a universal human propensity to invent diverse identities through choice-making. Further, such plural identities are themselves inherently historical; they are embodied in cultural forms of which it is necessarily true that they cross the generations, and that they distinguish themselves from other such cultural forms by the languages they speak, the values they acknowledge and other particularities by which their identities are constituted. From this point of view, a universal history, the history of the species as if it were a single organism, can be no more than a misleading metaphor.

If one aspect of Berlin's account of history is that there

cannot be a universal history of the species of the kind
aspired to by the Enlightenment *philosophes*, another is that
there cannot be 'laws of historical development', nor indeed
any science of history of which such laws are a part. Berlin's
denial that there are such laws follows on directly from
his rejection of determinism, and motivates his arguments
against historical inevitability. The very idea of a science of
history, according to Berlin, rests on a conception of human
beings, not as agents or choice-makers, but as natural objects
or processes, law-governed in their behaviours, and for that
reason predictable. As we have seen already, it is Berlin's
view that such a naturalistic or positivistic conception of
human beings does massive and underestimated violence to
our ordinary conception of ourselves. He asserts:

> If the belief in freedom – which rests on the assumption
> that human beings do occasionally choose, and that their
> choices are not wholly accounted for by the kind of causal
> explanations which are accepted in, say, physics or biol-
> ogy – if this is a necessary illusion, it is so deep and so
> pervasive that it is not felt as such. No doubt we can try
> to convince ourselves that we are systematically deluded;
> but unless we attempt to think out the implications of
> this possibility, and alter our modes of thought and
> speech to allow for it accordingly, this hypothesis remains
> hollow; that is, we find it impractical even to entertain
> it seriously, if our behaviour is to be taken as evidence of
> what we can and what we cannot bring ourselves to
> believe or suppose, not merely in theory, but in practice.
> My submission is that to make a serious attempt to adapt
> our thoughts and words to the hypothesis of determinism
> is a fearful task, as things are now, and have been within
> recorded history. The changes involved are very radical;
> our moral and psychological categories are, in the end,
> more flexible than our physical ones, but not much more
> so; it is not much easier to begin to think out in real
> terms, to which behaviour and speech would correspond,

what the universe of the genuine determinist would be like, than to think out, with the minimum of indispensable concrete detail (i.e. begin to imagine) what it would be like to be in a timeless world, or one with seventeen-dimensional space. Let those who doubt this try for themselves; the symbols with which we think will hardly lend themselves to the experiment; they, in their turn, are too deeply involved in our normal view of the world, allowing for every difference of period and clime and culture, to be capable of so violent a break.[3]

The obstacle involved in our adopting the perspective of determinism on human conduct is not, for Berlin, as it is for Popper, an epistemological obstacle: the difficulty that we cannot predict behaviour based on knowledge we do not now possess, but which future human beings may possess.[4] It is a conceptual, or, if you like, a metaphysical obstacle, created by our inability seriously or consistently to adopt a determinist self-conception, which would do away with our ordinary categories of thought about ourselves.

As seen by Berlin this obstacle can be expressed differently. We – our needs and so, in part, our natures – *are* our self-understanding. We may be deceived about ourselves, to be sure, but we cannot be *wholly* other than we suppose ourselves to be. Adopting a deterministic model of human beings entails, in effect, denying them the power of reflexive thought about themselves, the exercise of which informs choice-making, and introduces a partial indeterminacy into their nature. If human beings are engaged in self-creation through choice-making, then this is an activity which the adoption by them of a deterministic perspective on themselves would, according to Berlin, preclude or undermine. It is Berlin's clear view that this is an obstacle that no variant of compatibilism, not even dual-aspect theories of compatibilism, such as that proposed by Stuart Hampshire,[5] according to which causal and rational explanations of human behaviour are complementary rather than competitive, can overcome.

If choice and self-creation enter into human conduct at every point, then the conception of human beings as causally determined natural objects, invoked by the 'nomothetic' or 'covering law' account of historical explanation, according to which there are laws of historical development akin to the laws found in the natural sciences,[6] cannot be sustained. According to Berlin, two consequences follow from this. First, general theories of historical development which postulate laws – be they of progress or decline – are indefensible. Doctrines of historical inevitability are to be rejected for the same reason. It is not, to be sure, that there cannot be a 'situational logic' (in Popper's terminology)[7] which confers near-inevitability on certain outcomes; but there can be no long-term historical inevitabilities for entire societies, still less for the entire species. There can be a situational logic, only in so far as initial conditions are held in place; as these are altered, unpredictably, by human action, such logic loses application. Even where such situational logic applies, it does not yield inevitability, according to Berlin; for doctrines of historical inevitability presuppose the truth of determinism, in some version or other, and the applicability to human conduct of the nomological mode of explanation by general or universal laws of the sort found in the natural sciences.

It is just the use of the nomological model of explanation in history that Berlin thinks mistaken. For, secondly, contrary to Popper, Berlin asserts an irreducible diversity in method as between the natural sciences and the human studies, including history. Here we see Berlin applying his general position of methodological pluralism to the study of history by denying the applicability to history of models of explanation, nomological or teleological, that are appropriate in other areas of inquiry. Following Vico, he affirms that, when we study history, we are studying things that agents like ourselves have done and made; and the method appropriate to such study is one of imaginative empathy and reconstruction, not of nomological explanation. Berlin follows Vico, not only in asserting a fundamental discontinuity between the natural and the human sciences, but in affirming a method of inquiry – the method of empathy and imagination to which I have already referred – as being uniquely appropriate to the historical studies. For Berlin, then, history is a branch of knowledge that stands on its own feet, having a method that is peculiar to itself. It is clear that this conception of history as a discipline and as an object of knowledge is connected in Berlin with his view (shared by Vico) that the human species, unlike other animal species, is what it is partly by virtue of its understanding of its own past. Indeed, with Vico and (as we shall see) Marx, Berlin perceives that it is because the human species, unlike other animal species with which we are acquainted, is a partial self-creator, through choice-making and self-understanding, that it has a history at all. Biology is an appropriate model for the recurring cycles of animal species, but not for the self-transforming generations of human beings.

This view of human history separates Berlin's thought from any straightforwardly Humean naturalism, and leads us seriously to qualify Stuart Hampshire's interpretation of Berlinian liberalism as Humean:

> In all Berlin's thinking and writing one is aware of the ample, generous, humorous and seductive figure of David Hume smiling in the background. Hume's philosophy encourages the smooth transition from the mere description of normal human sentiments to the approval of such sentiments as Nature's provision for human welfare. We ought to follow Nature's guidance, and we make a serious mistake if we try to act against the natural and normal sentiments implanted in us. That is the way that leads to fanaticism, to false feeling and to dissimulation, and to a loss of self-assurance and of a clear sense of identity. So Hume, and after him, Berlin.[8]

Berlin's conception of the place of history in human affairs differs from Hume's far more than is allowed for in this account of it. In the first place Berlin, unlike Hume, conceives of human identities, individual as well as collective, as self-creations, never altogether fixed or finished, rather than as the natural effects of the admixture of a few human passions with changing circumstances. Notwithstanding Hume's account of the imagination, there is little in Hume of the view of human nature as in part always a self-creation, and of human history as being categorically different from any natural science. The project of a moral or social science, grounded in the constancies of human nature, that is announced in Hume's *Treatise*, is one to which Berlin has never subscribed, and which Hume never renounced.

A second way of stating the difference between Hume and Berlin is to note the regular or cyclical character of historical change in Hume's account of it. Since, for Hume, history is written in terms of the constancies of human nature, mediated through alterations in circumstances,[9] there is nothing of true novelty in Humean history, any more than there is in Machiavellian history. The categories of historical explanation are fixed, and simple: civilization and barbarism, rise and decline. History itself is conceived as the cyclical rise and fall of civilizations, and not – as, following Herder, Berlin conceives it – as the exfoliation of incommensurable cultures. It is doubtful if the very idea of a culture can be found in Hume's work, whether in his philosophical or his historical writings.

It is true that Hume and Berlin are alike in that neither subscribes to any Whiggish interpretation of history; but this is so for very different reasons. For Hume, moral improvement, and improvement in human knowledge, cannot be expected to be continuous, irreversible or permanent, since the natural condition of the human species militates against such progressive amelioration. Human benevolence and intelligence are fixed within narrow bounds, and it is in the natural course of human affairs that civilization should prove transitory, and that it should succumb to decadence or barbarism. For Berlin the interpretation of history in Whiggish terms of overall improvement or progress – however intermittent, interrupted, rare and subject to periods of regression – is rejected on the grounds of its incoherence, arising from the lack, in all but limiting cases, of any overarching standard whereby global progress or regress could be judged. It is not rejected by invoking a kind of pessimistic naturalism (of the sort found in Hume, Hobbes, or Spinoza). Such global, cross-cultural judgements of progress and regress may be feasible in the limiting case of the minimum content of core human values since, whatever conflicts they may issue in, we know of human societies, and historical milieux, in which all are compromised or violated. The human world is better if cruelty, the infliction of pain for purposes of pleasure alone, is diminished; and there are many societies – societies in which some human beings have the status of chattels whose well-being is of no account – which the minimum universal content of morality condemns outright. Such limiting cases aside, there are no transhistorical cross-cultural norms whereby global judgements of betterment or deterioration can meaningfully be made. Except in such cases, accordingly, interpretations of history in terms of fixed categories of civilization and barbarism, progress and decline, are unilluminating, and indeed dubiously meaningful.

One consequence of Berlin's repudiation of Enlightenment and Whiggish interpretations of history is worth noting here: that, whereas it does not allow of global, transhistorical judgements of progression and decline, save in limiting cases, it does enable us to recognize in history the occurrence of *loss* – of the disappearance of valuable achievements and activities that are dependent on doomed social and political structures, or systems of belief, for their existence or viability. This is only to acknowledge at the level of the lives of cultures and peoples what Berlin's account of radical choice emphasizes as true of the conduct of individuals: that it often involves, and involves unavoidably, irreparable losses of value, when incommensurably valuable options collide. In human history, such losses are often irreversible: valuable cultural forms are lost forever. They can be lost, except as traces left in cultural artefacts, partly because their practitioners are themselves historical creations. It is this historicity of human nature that at once disallows any conception of the advance of the entire species, and at the same time enables us to recognize as tragic the vanishing of irreplaceable cultural forms, whose value we can imaginatively recreate but cannot practically resurrect.

Like that of Herder and indeed Hegel, Berlin's account of human nature is historicist: most human goods (and evils) are conceived as historical creations, and human identities are seen as expressions of specific cultural forms, themselves historical creations. Here the comparison with Hegel, at any rate, ends. For Hegel, like his disciple Marx, human history had a teleological structure, its *telos* being human emancipation, the realization of the Absolute Idea, or *Geist*, or, in Marx's materialist restatement of this conception, the achievement of the post-historical communist society. Berlin rejects this (and every other) historical theodicy, as it is found in Hegel and Marx, in Burke, and even in Vico and Herder. Teleological categories apply in the explanation of purposive creatures, such as individual human beings; they have no application to human history as a whole. In this respect, Berlin's view is in direct contradiction with that of the Enlightenment *philosophes*, all of whom subscribed to a view of human history that was at once, and perhaps inconsistently, teleological and nomological. Berlin's opposition to this interpretation of history is partly philosophical, inasmuch as any such interpretation trades illicitly on providentialist or at least metaphysical assumptions – made explicit in the writings of Leibniz and Burke, for example, but not far below the surface in the works of Paine and Marx – in assuming a goal or end in human history for which there is no empirical warrant. Despite ingenious attempts to restate the Enlightenment interpretation of history without reference to such a *telos*,[10] teleological explanation is an indispensable element in the historical theodicy of the Enlightenment, as Berlin has repeatedly reminded us.[11]

There is also a normative and ethical motive which inspires his opposition to this kind of historical teleology. For in its inspired disciples and advocates, such as Hegel's Russian devotees – Belinsky, Bakunin, and many others – it produced a reification of historical forces, and a corresponding indifference or insensitivity to individual fates, against which any humanist sensibility must revolt. This must be so, whether or not these historical forces are supposed to be well disposed to the good of the human species as a whole, since in either case it is indifferent to that of mere individuals. In general, of course, theories of historical teleology (such as that of Marx) assume that the goal or inner purpose of history is benign – at least 'in the last resort' – but this is not always so, and in the most interesting historical teleologists this assumption is explicitly rejected or tacitly abandoned. The reification of historical forces, *without* the assumption of their ultimate beneficence, occurs in Tolstoy, of whom Berlin memorably writes:

> Tolstoy's central thesis – in some respects not unlike the inevitable 'self-deception' of the bourgeoisie held by his contemporary Karl Marx, save that what Marx reserves for a class, Tolstoy sees in almost all mankind – is that there is a natural law whereby the lives of human beings no less than that of nature are determined; but that men, unable to face this inexorable process, seek to represent it as a succession of free choices, to fix responsibility for what occurs upon persons endowed by them with heroic virtues or heroic vices, and called by them 'great men'. What are great men? They are ordinary human beings who are ignorant and vain enough to accept responsibility for the life of society, individuals who would rather take

the blame for all the cruelties, injustices, disasters justified in their name, than recognize their own insignificance and impotence in the cosmic flow which pursues its course irrespective of their wills and ideals.[12]

In Tolstoy, to be sure, this conviction of the reality of inexorable natural laws coexisted, inconsistently enough, with a programme of action, wholly at variance with the quietism that would seem more logically to follow from his Schopenhauerian fatalism: a programme of action concerned 'to discover, collect, expound eternal truths, awaken the spontaneous interest, the imagination, love, curiosity of children or simple folk, above all to liberate their "natural" moral, emotional and intellectual forces, which he did not doubt, as Rousseau did not doubt, would achieve harmony within men and between them . . .' Berlin comments on this Tolstoyan project:

> This programme – that of making possible the free self-development of all human faculties – rests on one vast assumption: that there exists at least one path of development on which these faculties will neither conflict with each other, nor develop disproportionately – a sure path to complete harmony in which everything fits and is at peace; with the corollary that knowledge of man's nature gained from observation or introspection or moral intuition, or from the study of the lives and writings of the best and wisest men of all ages, can show us this path.[13]

Thus it is that Tolstoy's 'programme of action' makes the heroic assumption, denied by Berlin's pluralism and by common human experience, but affirmed nevertheless in the mainstream of the Western tradition, that there is a path of development for mankind as a whole, if not for each of its individual members, in which all of its faculties and powers can be fully and harmoniously expressed. But it also amounts to a denial of these very historical forces, whose movements are inexorable and indifferent to our moral ideals, on which in his novels Tolstoy so adamantly insisted.

The reification of historical forces existed in Tolstoy in perpetual tension with a profound moral conviction of the goodness of 'natural man'. In most others, in Russia and elsewhere, the tension was too great to be maintained for long, and the tendency was to identify, in the manner of Hegel, the 'logic' of historical development with the destiny of the species, and to confer on this conjunction an ethical authority. Historical necessity and the moral imperative were then fused into one. Resistance to historical necessity in the name of ethical ideals, or for the sake of the vital interests of irreplaceable individuals, could then be ridiculed, as it was by Trotsky, as 'Quaker-vegetarian chatter'.[14] The abstract interest of universal humanity, as embodied in the necessities of its history, came then to displace concern for concrete individuals and their contingent fortunes. It did so, even in those whose initial inspiration was a love of individual liberty, such as Fichte. It led to the sacrifice of the present in favour of a supposedly predetermined future, that is so prominent a feature of twentieth-century political fanaticism.

It thereby supported a shift of concern from human beings in their inherited and partly self-created particularities to the requirements of abstract humanity. For one of the central tenets of the teleological view of history, especially in its Enlightenment variants, is the expectation of an eventual convergence of peoples on a universal civilization. This expectation of what might be called *the evanescence of particularism*[15] runs counter to the whole tendency of Berlin's Vichian account of the origin and nature of human self-identity as a form of self-creation, and to his celebration of cultural difference as expressive of what is most essential and universal in the human species. It goes against his view of human identities as always specific, never universal, however complex and plural they may be, and as being constituted, at any rate partly, by distinct historical narratives, recurrently recreated, in each generation. The Enlightenment ideal of a cosmopolitan civilization, in which particularistic attachments had been transcended or marginalized, is rejected by Berlin, and rejected explicitly,[16] as an impoverishment of the cultural diversity in which the incommensurable possibilities of human nature find their expression. It is not a state of affairs, supposing it to be achievable, that Berlin's pluralism encourages him to see as desirable.

It follows from all this that the Enlightenment interpretation of history as akin to the maturing of a single individual or organism, or as a series of stages or phases on the path to full human self-realization, that is found in Condorcet and Marx, say, embodies a false hypostatization of human nature that goes against the grain of Berlin's thought. Hampshire states the objection to this Enlightenment interpretation of history in terms that are largely acceptable to Berlin when he writes:

Hegelianism, positivism, Marxism, constructed in the shadow of Christianity with a view to its replacement, purported to give an account of the development of mankind as a whole, an account of the destiny of the species: this included an alienation or fall, followed by a political or social redemption, leading to a final salvation of humanity. From the standpoint of a naturalistic philosophy, looking at the so far known facts of human history, the gross implausibility of these accounts comes from the false speciation and the false humanism. 'Humanity' is either the name of a distinct animal species, with impressively distinct powers of mind and an uncertain future, or it is the name of a class of being constituted as distinct by the intention of its Creator; and of course the name may sometimes be used with both meanings in mind. If the supernatural claims about the Creator's intentions are dismissed, there remains no sufficient empirical reason to believe that there is such a thing as the historical development of mankind as a whole, unless the natural history of the evolution of the species is intended. What we see in history is the ebb and flow of different populations at different stages of social development, interacting with each other and exhibiting no common pattern of development. Using older historical categories, we can reasonably speak of the various populations flourishing and becoming powerful at some stage and then falling into decadence and becoming comparatively weak; and historians can reasonably look for some general causes of these rises and falls. Even if some such general causes can be found, they will not by themselves point to a destiny, and to an order of development, for mankind as a whole.[17]

Aside from its Humean naturalism, this is a view of history that corresponds closely to Berlin's. It has in common with the Humean naturalistic approach a suspicion of essentialist accounts of human nature and a reliance on empirical observation as an alternative to aprioristic reasoning about human beings.

What Berlin's account of human history emphasizes, and what is lacking in the Humean and naturalistic account given by Hampshire and in all varieties of Marxism, is the disposition of human beings to constitute for themselves particularistic identities, which Hampshire himself elsewhere stresses, when he criticizes Aristotle as follows:

Why did Aristotle, writing about the distinctive features of human beings, not mention the Babel of natural languages, the proliferation of religions with their exclusive customs and prohibitions, the attachment of populations to their separate and peculiar histories, the manifold frontiers and barriers, with the aid of which social groups and populations try to maintain that separate identity? Why

did he not see this species-wide divisiveness, the drive
to separateness and conflicting identities, as at least one
distinctive feature of human beings among all the animal
species?[18]

It is not only the propensity to cultural difference that seems
lacking in Hume, in Aristotle, and in Marx, but also the
recognition that cultural forms are modes of human self-
expression, exteriorizations of human identity in which its
constitutive elements, themselves always discrete and particular, are deposited. In a recent statement Hampshire has
criticized the belief in the epiphenomenal and transitory
character of particularistic human identities as arising from
'the belief in a positivist theory of modernization, a theory
that is traceable to the French Enlightenment. The positivists believed that all societies across the globe will gradually
discard their traditional attachments to supernatural forces
because of the need for rational, scientific and experimental
methods of thought which a modern industrial economy
involves. This is the old faith, widespread in the nineteenth
century, that there must be a step-by-step convergence on
liberal values, on "our values". We now know that there is
no "must" about it and that all such theories of human
history have a predictive value of zero. They are all just
diachronic versions of the Platonic belief in a final rational
harmony.'[19] Here the positivist chimera of a convergence on
a single universal civilization, and a single form of human
identity, is rejected on grounds fully acceptable to Berlin.
That human identities are, and cannot be other than, local
and particular in their natures, is an implication of Berlin's
Vichian and Herderian account of the historicity of human
nature that goes very much against the grain of the mainstream Western tradition, and of its flowering in the European Enlightenment.

It is Berlin's rejection of the Enlightenment idea that cultural diversity is transitory or even epiphenomenal in history, together with his criticism of the reification of

historical forces and the ascription to them of an ethical authority that, at least as much as his repudiation of historical inevitability, is at the bottom of his opposition to Marxism. In his early and brilliantly evocative study, *Karl Marx*, first published in 1939, Berlin is clear that Marx's system of thought depends on metaphysical presuppositions that remain indefensible despite Marx's own attempt to give his theory of history systematic empirical corroboration. As Berlin puts his view of Marx's system of ideas: 'The laws of history were indeed eternal and immutable – and to grasp this fact a quasi-metaphysical intuition was required – but what they were could be established only by the evidence of empirical facts. His intellectual system was a closed one, everything that entered was made to conform to a pre-established pattern, but it was grounded in observation and experience.'[20] Berlin reiterates the dependency of the Marxian system on metaphysical assumptions later in the book, as follows:

> The central Hegelian conception remains at the basis of Marx's thought, though it is transposed into semi-empirical terms. History is not the succession of the effects on men of external environment or of their own unalterable constitutions, or even the interplay between these factors, as earlier materialists had supposed. Its essence is the struggle of men to realize their full human potentialities; and, since they are members of the natural kingdom (for there is nothing that transcends it), man's effort to realize himself fully is a striving to escape from being the plaything of forces that seem at once mysterious, arbitrary and irresistible, that is, to attain mastery of them and of himself, which is freedom. Man attains this subjugation of his world not by increasing knowledge obtained by contemplation (as Aristotle had supposed) but by activity, by labour, the conscious moulding by men of their environment and of each other ... Labour transforms man's world, and himself too, in the course of its

activity. Some needs are more basic than others – bare survival comes before more sophisticated wants. But man differs from the animals, with whom he shares essential physical needs, in possessing the gift of invention; thereby he alters his own nature and its needs, and escapes from the repetitive cycles of the animals, who remain unaltered and therefore have no history. The history of society is the history of the inventive labours that alter man, alter his desires, habits, outlook, relationships both to other men and to physical nature, with which man is in perpetual physical and technological metabolism.[21]

These passages bring out part, at least, of what Berlin finds objectionable in the Marxian interpretation of history – its ultimate dependency on metaphysical premises, including an essentialist view of man. Presupposed by such passages, and by similar ones elsewhere in Berlin's writings, is the claim that Marx was, indeed, a historical determinist – a claim which I find eminently plausible, but which I cannot here examine or comment upon, except to say that it is one to which latter-day Marxists will immediately (and predictably) object. Less obvious than these familiar contrasts between Berlin and Marx are some points of interesting similarity and affinity between their views that such passages suggest. Both Berlin and Marx conceive of man as a self-transforming being whose needs alter as his self-understanding changes and who does not have a history by accident, as perhaps human beings do in some materialist and Kantian conceptions of them, but constitutively. In this affirmation of the historicity of human nature Marx and Berlin are at one. They differ, most obviously, in Berlin's rejection of the teleological conception of history, and indeed of the world, he attributes to Marx. As Berlin remarks,

The notion that history obeys laws, whether natural or supernatural, that every event of human life is an element in a necessary pattern, has deep metaphysical origins: infatuation with the natural sciences feeds this stream, but is not its sole nor, indeed, its principal source. In the first place, there is the teleological outlook whose roots reach back to the beginnings of human thought ... In this cosmology the world of men (and, in some versions, of the entire universe) is a single all-inclusive hierarchy; so that to explain why each ingredient of it is as it is, and where, and when it is, and does what it does, is *eo ipso* to say what its goal is, how far it successfully fulfils it, and what are the relations of co-ordination and subordination between the goals of the various goal-pursuing entities in the harmonious pyramid which they collectively form. If this is a true picture of reality, then historical explanation, like every other form of explanation, must consist, above all, of the attribution to individuals, groups, nations, species, of their proper place in a universal pattern.[22]

Berlin concludes: 'This attitude is profoundly anti-empirical.'[23]

It is plain from the context of this and similar statements that Berlin's objection to teleological interpretations of history, that they depend on metaphysical premises and are never defensible empirically, applies in his view fully to Marxism. He claims also that Marx collapses historical necessity into moral authority:

The only sense in which it is possible to show that something is good or bad, right or wrong, is by demonstrating that it accords or discords with the historical process – the collective progressive activity of men – that it assists it or thwarts it, will survive or will inevitably perish. All causes permanently lost or doomed to fail, in the complex but historically determined ascent of mankind, are, by that very fact, made bad and wrong, and indeed this is what constitutes the meaning of such terms.[24]

That Marx commits a fallacy of ethical naturalism of this sort, in which a moral term is given a wholly descriptive meaning, is denied by defenders of Marx such as G. A. Cohen, who point to passages in his works where the distinction between fact and value elided or conflated in such fallacies seems to be clearly recognized.[25] Berlin's argument against Marxism, that it contains a historical teleology for which there can be no empirical warrant, still stands, and if valid is by itself fatal to the Marxian system.

Berlin's deepest objection to the Marxian system seems to me, however, to be the one he makes least explicitly – an objection to the *content* of Marx's historical teleology. For the implication of Marxian historical materialism is that cultural difference is epiphenomenal and will disappear from human life with the passing of class societies; or, if it survives, that it will do so in marginal and unimportant forms. Thus, although Marx nowhere commits himself to the view that national cultures will vanish in a communist society, everything he writes, together with the distinction between base and superstructure that is integral to his historical materialism, suggests that he took it for granted that if national cultures did survive the passing of class society, it would be in forms that – like ethnic cuisines in our own day, perhaps – lack political significance. So, according to Marx, even if this key variety of cultural difference, differences in national culture, were a feature of communist society, it could not be an occasion of war, revolution, or other deep social divisions.

Marx is a paradigmatic Enlightenment thinker, then, in subscribing to the doctrine of the evanescence of particularism, at least in the forms in which it is politically important and is an occasion of social division. The naturalistic anthropology that underlies this doctrine is one that Berlin rejects, even if he approves of those of its aspects – those in which it conceives of man as a self-transforming creature – in which it deviates from the most primitive forms of Enlightenment materialism. He rejects this naturalistic anthropology, because it rests on a metaphysical premise according to which the human essence is what is universal in man, *Gattungswesen*, or species-being; where the content of the human essence is the capacity for co-operative, creative labour. It is this account of the human essence that underlies Marx's theory of alienation and is the ultimate basis for Marxian ethics. In contrast, in Berlin's view, as in Herder's, the human essence – if there is such a thing – is best expressed in cultural difference, in the propensity to fashion diverse forms of life with their divergent conceptions of flourishing. No single conception of flourishing, such as the Marxian conception of self-realization through co-operative and creative labour, can on the Berlinian and Herderian view claim to be the unique, the best or the most privileged embodiment of the human essence. A form of life in which human beings found fulfilment through co-operative labour might be a genuine example of human flourishing; but it would always be only one, with other cultural forms embodying others. It is a feature of Marxism, however, along with other Enlightenment ideologies, that it privileges its particular view of flourishing with the claim – backed up by a philosophy of history – that it alone expresses the human essence. This is the claim, most centrally constitutive both of the Enlightenment and of the classical Western tradition, that Berlin most decisively rejects. Berlin's deepest reason for rejecting Marxism, therefore, is that Marxism is a species – perhaps the boldest, if not also the most plausible – of the Enlightenment anthropology he rejects. And the view he endorses, in which it is the propensity to cultural difference that is most essentially human, may be taken as the radical anthropological form of his value-pluralism.

The distance between Humean or Marxian naturalism, and Berlin's Herderian expressivism about cultural forms, is particularly evident in the conception of language Berlin attributes to Herder,[26] and to which he himself evidently largely subscribes. This is a conception which is wholly at odds with the designative model of language-use that dominates English empiricism from Bacon and Locke to Hobbes and Hume, and, in our own day, Russell and Ayer.[27] For, whereas in the designative view, whose limiting-case expression may perhaps be found in Wittgenstein's *Tractatus*, language is an instrument for conveying independently occurring ideas, or mirroring or representing an independently existing world, in the expressivist view our thoughts and activities are already linguistic, so to speak, they are *au fond* saturated with language, and the project of prising words from the world is a hopeless one.[28] For the expressivist view, in other words, an instrumentalist view of language as a neutral medium in which pre-linguistic realities are captured or transmitted – the designative view, in short – is fundamentally misconceived. On the contrary, languages are seen themselves as forms of life. And, in the Herderian expressivism that Berlin himself endorses, these forms of life are always particular, never universal in their content. It may well be that the idea of a *culture*, which I have speculated is not to be found in Hume, is no older than the expressivist conception of language.

The idea of cultural forms as deposits for human identities is, at any rate, wholly lacking in Hume, as is the conception of cultural forms as exteriorizations of human will, which Berlin finds in Fichte.[29] The deepest divergence of Berlin from Hume, however, and, for that matter, from Marx, comes in the self-transformative power Berlin attributes to human choice-making, in which he is at one with Romantic voluntarism, though with decisive reservations.[30] It is clear that Romantic expressivism and voluntarism both strengthen Berlin's pluralism in ways that are bound to undermine the philosophical anthropology of the Enlightenment. This is so, even if Berlin's expressivism and his voluntarism do not always pull in the same direction. It remains true, even if Berlin's agonistic liberalism seeks to retain Enlightenment commitments to human emancipation while relinquishing the delusive anthropology on which they were historically founded.

A crucial question to be considered, accordingly, is whether these Enlightenment commitments can survive the destruction of their foundations in philosophical anthropology that in various forms underpinned them in the *philosophes* and their disciples, such as Marx. If human beings are self-transforming creatures whose forms of life, values and identities are essentially plural, what is it that elevates the life of liberal reason – the life of choice and self-criticism – over all others? If fundamental human values are incommensurables, will this not also be true of the value of choice? If there is the deep value-conflict marked by the idea of incommensurability, what can justify according negative freedom even a general priority over other, competing political goods? We have seen already that – as Berlin candidly acknowledges[31] – Machiavelli draws no liberal moral from his assertion of the pluralism of virtues and of moralities; it is no less relevant that his conception of liberty is not negative, but (as Quentin Skinner has shown)[32] positive, that of collective self-rule. What could achieve the result in which liberalism is privileged?

A related question is whether Enlightenment commitments to the growth of knowledge and to human emancipation can survive the abandonment of the philosophical anthropology and conception of human history on which they were grounded. Before these questions can be considered, however, we must examine in greater depth Berlin's reasons for repudiating Enlightenment understandings of man's nature and history. It is partly the universal human disposition to cultural difference that grounds Berlin's rejection of Enlightenment philosophies of history. And it is this disposition which is invoked in his account of the political embodiment of particularistic self-identity – which the *philosophes* supposed to be a transitory phase in man's historical development – which he recognizes in our time as nationalism.

4 Nationalism

... What is here entailed is that the highest ends for which men have rightly striven and sometimes died are strictly incompatible with one another. Even if it were possible to revive the glories of the past as those pre-historicist thinkers (Machiavelli or Mably, for instance) thought, who called for a return to the heroic virtues of Greece or Rome, we could not revive and unite them all. If we choose to emulate the Greeks, we cannot also emulate the Hebrews; if we model ourselves on the Chinese, whether as they are in reality, or in Voltaire's *opéra bouffe* version, we cannot also be the Florentines of the Renaissance, or the innocent, serene, hospitable savages of the eighteenth-century imagination. Even if, *per impossibile*, we could choose among these ideals, which should we select? Since there is no common standard in terms of which to grade them, there can be no final solution to the problem of what men as such should aim at. The supposition that this question can, at least in principle, be answered correctly and finally, which few had seriously doubted since Plato had taken it for granted, is undermined. Herder, of course, condemns the very wish to resurrect ancient ideals: ideals belong to the form of life which generates them, and are mere historical memories without them. Values – ends – live and die with the social wholes of which they form an intrinsic part. Each 'collective individuality' is unique, and has its own aims and standards, which will themselves inevitably be superseded by other goals and values – ethical, social and aesthetic. Each of these systems is objectively valid in its own day, in the course of 'Nature's long year' which brings all things to pass. All cultures are equal in the sight of God, each in its time and place. Ranke said precisely this: his theodicy is a complacent version of Herder's theses, directed equally against those of Hegel and moral scepticism. But if this is so, then the notion of the perfect civilization in which the ideal human being realizes his full potentialities is patently absurd: not merely difficult to formulate, or impossible to realize in practice, but incoherent and unintelligible. This is perhaps the sharpest blow ever delivered against the classical philosophy of the West, to which the notion of perfection – the possibility, at least in principle, of universal, timeless solutions of problems of value – is essential.

Isaiah Berlin, 'Herder and the Enlightenment'[1]

One of the most significant aspects of Berlin's treatment of nationalism is its recurrence to an older, and in many ways a wiser, tradition of liberal thought. Nineteenth-century European liberal thinkers, by contrast with their Enlightenment predecessors and their twentieth-century successors, grasped the importance to human beings of collective identities other than, and more particularistic than, that of the species as a whole. It is a feature of the thought of Benjamin Constant, of Alexis de Tocqueville, of John Stuart Mill, for example, that they perceived in the sentiment of nationality an important source of social solidarity, and of the political stability of a liberal society. By contrast with twentieth-century liberals, such as Hayek and Popper, for whom nationalism is only tribalism revived and written large, these nineteenth-century liberals grasped the significance of membership in a common culture in sustaining allegiance to a liberal political order. Almost alone among twentieth-century liberal thinkers, with Joseph Raz being virtually the only significant exception, Berlin continues this older liberal tradition, which associated itself with the human need for a common culture, and recognized its principal political embodiment in modern times in the nation-state. Further, along with Raz, Berlin perceives that a liberal civil society cannot rest upon abstract principles or common rules alone, but needs a common national culture[2] if it is to be stable and command allegiance. In this respect Berlin and Raz renew an unjustly neglected aspect of J. S. Mill's liberalism, that in which he emphasized the importance of the sentiment of nationality in a liberal culture.[3]

In common with all liberal thinkers, Berlin repudiates the pathology of nationalist sentiment, so common in our century, as alien to central liberal values of toleration and human dignity. By contrast with the dominant schools of liberal thought in the post-war world – the neo-Austrian school, embracing Popper and Hayek, as well as the Anglo-American school of Rawls and Dworkin – Berlin sees in nationality the modern expression of a human disposition that appears to be universal and immemorial – the disposition to develop a specific and particularistic identity. Indeed, again by contrast with the dominant forms of post-war liberalism, he perceives that participation in common cultural forms and membership of communities that are self-governing or at least autonomous in their own affairs, are vital elements in human flourishing for the vast majority of the species. He has never subscribed to the belief that human dignity and self-esteem depend solely on the possession of individual rights and liberties; they depend also, though separately, on freedom from the oppression to which each of us may be subject as the member of a specific people or the practitioner of a particular cultural tradition. Throughout the long and terrible history of Christian anti-Semitism, for example, it is true that Jews were oppressed by being denied negative liberties assured to others; but they were oppressed, also, as Jews, by attempts at forcible conversion, and the many other attacks on their identity as Jews, which, even before the Holocaust, provided powerful reasons for the establishment of a national Jewish homeland. In other words, dignity and self-esteem depend for the vast majority of human beings not only on the enjoyment of negative liberties but also on their distinctive values and form of life being embodied in the social and political institutions to which they are subject. Human beings need to have their particular identities and forms of life reflected or mirrored, in forms recognizable to them, in the institutions of their societies. If this is denied them, they will lack an essential element of human dignity, even if they possess negative liberty to the highest degree, for they will be unable to recognize themselves, to see themselves reflected, in the institutions that confer negative liberty upon them. Further, the well-being of individuals cannot be dissociated from the flourishing of the common cultural forms to which they belong: the very options from which they choose, and most of the goods they pursue, are constituted by these forms, and individual well-being is impoverished to the extent that they are in disrepair. Finally, and for our purposes perhaps most importantly, the ways of life, or common cultural forms, to which human beings are attached, and from membership of which their identities are derived, have the constitutive characteristics of inherent plurality and mutual exclusivity. They are many, not one, and though they may coexist and influence one another they cannot commingle without losing their identities as distinct ways of life. This is the application, or implication, of the value-pluralist idea of the uncombinability of goods and virtues to whole ways of life – that they are typically exclusive of one another. (This is not to say that they are easy to individuate, that people do not sometimes belong to several cultures or migrate from one to another, that common forms of life do not develop reciprocal or dialectical relationships between one another, and so forth.) The upshot of these points is that, for Berlin, individual well-being is so bound up with participation in common cultural forms as to be barely conceivable apart from them.

It is a mistake, for this reason, to interpret Berlin's defence of negative liberty, or his liberalism in general, in terms of the individualist conception of human well-being in which the human good can be cashed out in private satisfactions. On the contrary, Berlin is at one with the communitarian critics of liberalism in affirming that there is an ineliminable public or communal dimension of individual well-being for all, or almost all, human beings. Where, like Joseph Raz, he

differs from the communitarian thinkers is in his conviction
that liberal practices and communal forms can and should be
reconciled with one another, balanced as equally legitimate
aspects of human well-being, answers to different but no
less profound human needs.

Berlin's points of affinity with, and differences from, the
communitarian critics of liberalism may be put in another
way, by reference to the communitarian idea of the 'situated'
or 'embedded' self. This idea, formulated clearly in the writings of Michael Sandel and deployed powerfully in the work
of Alasdair MacIntyre and Charles Taylor,[4] holds against
the abstract individualism of much liberal theory that the
relations of the self or subject with its projects and attachments are not instrumental but constitutive. We are not
free-floating Kantian subjects, for which every relationship
is revocable and no form of common life definitive; we find
ourselves embedded in relationships and attachments which
enter into and shape our very identities. With all of this
Berlin concurs. To do political philosophy as if it were an
accident that human beings have histories, as do recent Kantian liberals such as Rawls and Dworkin, who are the principal objects of communitarian criticism, is to make ciphers
– not human beings, whose very essences are historical –
its subject matter. For Berlin as for the communitarians this
is a grievous error. Where Berlin parts company with the
communitarians, at least at their most radical, is in his rejection of the idea – present in the work both of Sandel and
MacIntyre – of the 'radically situated self' – the human subject, that is to say, whose identity is formed by membership
of a single moral community. It is plain to Berlin that this
is, at best, an ideal type, to which virtually no one – certainly
no one in the modern world – conforms. Further, it is a
dangerous idea, in its own way as much of an abstraction
as the idea of the Kantian subject that is dispossessed of all
constitutive attachments. For, if it is true that none of us is
or could be such a Kantian subject, it is no less true that
none of us is a radically situated subject. We all – all of us,

at any rate, who belong to a modern culture, and live in a modern society – have plural allegiances, belong to diverse communities, and know the experience of conflicting roles. Plurality and conflict are integral to our identities. Both the left-wing and the right-wing communitarian versions of the ideal of an integral or organic community flout this fact of the complexity and conflict which is the inheritance of all of us. It is its insensitivity to the fact of diversity within our very identities which distinguishes the communitarian criticism of liberalism from Berlin's communitarian liberalism.

It is important to note what is, and what is not, implied by Berlin's affirmation of the importance, indeed the necessity, of common cultural forms to individual human well-being. He is not endorsing the civic humanist or classical republican view, revived in our time by Hannah Arendt, that human flourishing demands political participation. This belief he rejects, despite its distinguished Aristotelian pedigree. He rejects it, no doubt in part in virtue of his very pluralism – his conviction that there is no single activity, or hierarchy of activities, by reference to which the diversity of forms of human flourishing can be circumscribed. Neither contemplation nor political activity can be the supreme end of human life, since there is no such thing. It is in any case not political participation, but membership in common cultural traditions, that Berlin thinks essential to most forms of human flourishing. As Stuart Hampshire describes Berlin's view:

> Berlin has argued with great force that Enlightenment thinkers who looked forward to men and women becoming citizens of an undivided world were deceived. Herder, Hamann and Hume were, in their different ways, right to represent persons as governed in their thoughts and sentiments by the habits and customs in which they were nurtured, and not by rational principles demanding universal agreement. Vico was right to assert against

Descartes that natural languages, and civilization itself in
its many forms, are the products of imagination and of
poetic invention and of metaphor, and not of abstract
reasoning and of clear and distinct ideas. Clear and distinct
ideas are accessible to all humanity; the idioms of a natural
language are not . . . In the last analysis, a sane nationalism
is to be justified by a utilitarian argument – that most men
and women are happy only when their way of life prolongs
customs and habits which are familiar to them.[5]

What is essential to human well-being, for Berlin, is not
participation in any political unit, say that of the nation-
state, but participation in a 'collective individuality', a
common form of cultural life, having its own history, habits
and arts, its own vernacular and distinctive idioms of activity. Such forms of common cultural life cannot always be
readily individuated; and this is *one* reason why Berlin does
not subscribe to the doctrine of integral or organic nationalism, expounded by reactionary thinkers such as Maurras,
who maintain that national cultures should be homogenous,
and coterminous with sovereign states. Another reason is
that he acknowledges that we are many of us bearers of
plural inheritances – a fact which makes the proposition
that we are, or ought to be, members of a single moral community, itself defining a single political unit, divisive and
dangerous, whether it is advanced by reactionaries or left-
wing communitarians. This radical and reactionary doctrine
of nationalism is one Berlin has never endorsed.

Berlin gives an explicit statement of what he understands
by nationalism when he tells us:

By nationalism, I mean something more definite, ideo-
logically important and dangerous [than 'national sentiment as such – that can probably be traced to tribal feeling
in the earliest period of recorded history']: namely, the
conviction, in the first place, that men belong to a particular human group, and that the way of life of the group

differs from that of others; that the characters of the individuals who compose the group are shaped by, and cannot be understood apart from, those of the group, defined in terms of common history, customs, laws, memories, beliefs, language, artistic and religious expressions, social institutions, ways of life, to which some add heredity, kinship, racial characteristics; and that it is these factors which shape human beings, their purposes and their values.

Secondly, that the pattern of life of a society is similar to that of a biological organism; that what this organism needs for its proper development, which those most sensitive to its nature articulate in words or images or other forms of human expression, constitutes its common goals; that these goals are supreme; in cases of conflict with other values, which do not derive from the specific ends of a specific 'organism' – intellectual or religious or moral, personal or universal – these supreme values should prevail, since only so will the decadence and ruin of the nation be averted. Furthermore, that to call such patterns of life organic is to say that they cannot be artificially formed by individuals or groups, however dominating their positions, unless they are themselves penetrated by these historically developing ways of acting and thinking and feeling, for it is these mental and emotional and physical ways of living, of coping with reality, above all the ways in which human beings deal with one another, that determine everything else and constitute the national organism – the nation – whether it takes the form of a state or not. Whence it follows that the essential human unit in which man's nature is fully realized is not the individual, or a voluntary association which can be dissolved or altered or abandoned at will, but the nation; that it is to the creation and maintenance of the nation that the lives of subordinate units, the family, the tribe, the clan, the province, must be due, for their nature and purpose, what is often called their meaning, are derived from its nature and its purposes; and that these are revealed not by rational analysis, but by a special awareness, which need not be fully conscious, of the unique relationship that binds individual human beings into the indissoluble and unanalysable organic whole which Burke identified with society, Rousseau with the people, Hegel with the state, but which for nationalists is, and can only be, the nation, whatever its social structure or form of government.

Thirdly, this outlook entails the notion that one of the most compelling reasons, perhaps the most compelling, for holding a particular belief, pursuing a particular policy, serving a particular end, living a particular life, is that these ends, beliefs, policies, lives, are *ours*. This is tantamount to saying that these rules or doctrines or principles should be followed not because they lead to virtue or happiness or justice or liberty, or are ordained by God or church or prince or parliament or some other universally acknowledged authority, or are good or right in themselves, and therefore valid in their own right, universally, for all men in a given situation; rather they are to be followed because these values are those of *my* group – for the nationalist, of *my* nation; these thoughts, feelings, this course of action, are good or right, and I shall achieve fulfilment or happiness by identifying myself with them, because they are demands of the particular form of social life into which I have been born, to which I am connected by Burke's myriad strands, which reach into the past and future of my nation, and apart from which I am, to change the metaphor, a leaf, a twig, broken off from the tree, which alone can give it life; so that if I am separated from it by circumstance or my own wilfulness, I shall become aimless, I shall wither away, being left, at best, with nostalgic memories of what it once was to have been truly alive and active, and performing that function in the pattern of the national life, understanding of which alone gave meaning and value to all I was and did.[6]

Berlin's understanding of nationalism, though it is at a great remove from that of reactionary radical theorists such as Maurras, is of a piece with his rejection of the philosophical anthropology of the Enlightenment, for which cultural difference was not of the essence of humanity, but something ephemeral, or at least evanescent, a phase in human development, not constitutive of humanity itself. For Berlin, individual self-creation occurs always in a context of common cultural forms, but these are always *particular* forms, not the inheritance of all mankind. They are particular as individual histories, and the plurality of natural languages, are particular. There is a deep difference between the communitarian aspect of Berlin's liberalism and the vision of community, egalitarian and universal, that animates most latter-day communitarian critics of liberalism. Their community is an ideal form, not a historic practice, not a community human beings have ever lived in, it is a form of community from which the contingencies of natural language and cultural difference have been purged, so that only the elements of abstract universal humanity remain. This is, in effect, not a community at all, but rather an association of ciphers. To say this is to say that, even if the ideal of equality is prized – as it is by Berlin, among other political goods – its achievement will be its embodiment in the life of a historic human community, not the erection of an ideal community from which all particularistic contingencies have been expunged.

Whereas Berlin shares with the communitarian critics of liberalism the conviction that individual well-being presupposes rich common cultural forms, his suspicion appears to be that the individual whose well-being is identified with that of a universal community is a denatured abstraction, not to be found in the real world of history and common experience. In this real world, individuals are constituted by their particularities, what is most essentially constitutive of them is what is most contingent and accidental – their place and time of birth, their first language and family lineage, the cultural tradition by which they are formed and whose power over them is shown in the very act of rebellion against it. It is because of the diversity of particular human identities, each of them distinctive and irreducible to any other, that Berlin recognizes to be a defining feature of our species, that he is able to reject both the abstract individualism of liberal rationalism and the conceptions of organic social unity that distinguish radical critics of liberalism of both the Left and the Right. Berlin's communitarian liberalism, if one may so call it, is for these reasons necessarily pluralistic and respectful of the conflicts that particular complex human identities will occasion in society, and even within individuals.

Nationalism is connected with the human need for a particular identity in another way – as the search for recognition, which Hegel explored powerfully in his analysis of *Anerkennung*. Our identities are not free-standing entities, in need of no confirmation by the world; they are partly constituted, sometimes against our own wills, by recognition by others. If a man of Jewish lineage seeks to deny his identity as a Jew, and to claim the identity of the people to which he has assimilated, he may succeed from his own point of view; but he may nevertheless find his ancestral identity as a Jew imposed upon him, regardless of his own self-conception, by elements in the larger community of which he is, or believes himself to be, a member. For him, if he has the misfortune to find himself in the France of the Dreyfus affair or of the Pétain regime, in the Germany of the National Socialists or the Russia of the Black Hundreds, to be a Jew is his fate, from which the adoption of a self-chosen identity, by assimilation, offers no escape. There is here a limit on the possibilities of individual self-creation that is imposed by others, and by the contingencies of history. It is a theme to which I shall return, later in this chapter, when I come to consider Berlin's attitude to Zionism.

For the most part, it is not in the denial of the opportunity of escape from a historically given identity, through chosen assimilation to another, that the importance of the need for recognition in the generation of nationalism is to be found. It is in the simple denial of recognition, by humiliation or conquest, by cultural imperialism, whether ethnic in inspiration (as in the Russifying policies of the last Tsars) or universalist in its self-conception (as with French cultural imperialism in the eighteenth century), or by the many forms of national subjugation and annexation, that the human need for recognition is thwarted. It was in a reaction to French universalism, the form in which French cultural imperialism was perceived by them, that the German theorists of populism, and above all J. G. Herder, developed their account of the 'collective individuality' that was a necessary precondition of individual flourishing. In this they tended to confirm Schiller's interpretation of the assertion of national culture as akin to a 'bent twig', a response to national humiliation, military, political, or – most subtly corrosive – cultural. This account of the pathology of the modern nationalism as a reactive phenomenon – suggested by Schiller, and endorsed by Berlin – seems to be only further corroborated by twentieth-century experience – by the Weimar tragedy, and its echoes in other places and times, such as contemporary Russia, where the experience of national humiliation and imperial dissolution has given a further lease on life to the reactionary demagogues of *Pamyat*, Vladimir Zhirinovsky's misnamed Liberal Democratic Party, and similar organizations. It is arguable that the phenomenon of fundamentalism, in Iran and elsewhere, is analogously reactive, a reassertion of a cultural identity that has already been altered, or even shattered, by the forces of modernization.

The *lumières* of the Enlightenment, and their followers in our century, consistently underestimated the significance of cultural difference, and its political embodiment in nationalism, because they subscribed to a philosophical anthropology for which particularism was epiphenomenal and so fated to be peripheral or marginal, and rarely, if ever, a decisive political force in the future of human affairs. As Berlin puts it:

> No social or political thinker in the nineteenth century was unaware of nationalism as a dominant movement of his age. Nevertheless, in the second half of the century, indeed up to the First World War, it was thought to be waning. Consciousness of national identity may well be as old as social consciousness itself. But nationalism, unlike liberal feeling or xenophobia, seems scarcely to have existed in ancient or classical times. There were other foci of collective loyalty. It seems to emerge at the end of the Middle Ages in the West, particularly in France, in the form of the defence of customs and privileges of localities, regions, corporations, and, of course, states, and then of the nation itself, against the encroachment of some external power – Roman law or papal authority – or against related forms of universalism – natural law and other claims of supranational authority. Its emergence as a coherent doctrine may perhaps be placed and dated in the last third of the eighteenth century in Germany, more particularly in the conceptions of the *Volksgeist* and *Naturalgeist* in the writings of the vastly influential poet and philosopher Johann Gottfried Herder.[7]

In misunderstanding cultural difference, and thereby the political significance of collective identification, all of the twentieth-century ideologies of Enlightenment failed to confront the most powerful – and, in many ways, the most destructive – forces of the age. It is a distinctive feature of Berlin's liberal outlook that, while remaining steadfastly committed to Enlightenment values of toleration, liberty and human emancipation from ignorance and oppression, it rejects the Enlightenment conception which sees universalizing reason as the mark of man, and a rational society, in which particularism has been transcended or else domesticated, as the *telos*, the aim, goal, or end of history. In locating the most centrally constitutive mark of the species in the capacity for self-creation through choice-making, and in perceiving each of the diversity of identities so created to be particularistic in its essence, Berlin's thought reveals its affinity with that of the Romantics, which I consider in the next chapter.

We may uncover some of the distinctive claims and presuppositions of Berlin's account of nationalism by comparing it with the illuminating philosophical analysis of national self-determination advanced by Joseph Raz and Avishai Margalit.[8] They suggest six characteristics that in combination are relevant to a case for self-determination for a group. The first is that a group 'has a common character and a common culture that encompass many, varied and important aspects of life, a culture that defines or marks a variety of forms or styles of life, types of activities, occupations, pursuits and relationships. With national groups we expect to find national cuisines, distinctive architectural styles, a common language, distinctive literary and artistic traditions, national music, customs, dress, ceremonies and holidays, etc.' The second is that 'people growing up among members of the group will acquire the group culture, will be marked by its character . . . given the pervasive nature of the culture of the groups we are seeking to identify, their influence on individuals who grow up in their midst is profound and far-reaching. The point needs to be made in order to connect concern with the prosperity of the group with concern for the well-being of individuals. This tie between the individual and the collective is at the heart of the case for self-determination.' Thirdly, 'Membership in the group is, in part, a matter of mutual recognition.' Typically, one belongs to such groups if, among other conditions, one is recognized by other members of the group as belonging to it. Fourthly, '. . . membership of such groups is an important identifying feature for each about himself. These are groups, members of which are aware of their membership and typically regard it as an important clue in understanding who they are, in interpreting their actions and reactions, in understanding their tastes and their manners.' Fifthly, 'membership is a matter of belonging, not of achievement. One does not have to prove oneself, or to excel in anything, in order to belong and to be accepted as a full member. To the extent that membership normally involves recognition by others as a member, that recognition is not conditional on meeting qualifications that indicate any accomplishment.' Sixthly, the groups concerned 'are anonymous groups where mutual recognition is secured by the possession of general characteristics . . . given the importance of mutual recognition to members of these groups, they tend to develop conventional means of identification, such as the use of symbolic objects, participation in group ceremonies, special group manners, or special vocabulary, which help to identify quickly who is "one of us" and who is not.'[9]

The relevance to, and parallelism with, Berlin's account of the sources of nationalism of Margalit's and Raz's analysis is clear and worth enlarging upon. The most important points are the pervasive influence on individuals of common forms of cultural life and the intimate link this establishes between individual well-being and the prosperity of forms of common life, the role participation in common cultural forms plays in forming the self-conception of individuals, and the significance of recognition by others in confirming membership in forms of common life. These points of affinity are present, and if anything more pronounced in a subsequent paper by Raz on 'Multiculturalism: A Liberal Perspective'.[10] In this later paper Raz stresses the constitutive links between individual well-being and participation in common cultural forms in terms that run parallel to the account Berlin gives of their relations. Raz's stress on the mutually constitutive relations between the well-being of individuals and the flourishing of cultures acquires a deeper, and perhaps a tragic meaning, with many echoes in Berlin's writings, when he goes on to explore the connections between value-pluralism and the agonistic exclusivity of common cultural forms. As Raz puts it:

... conflict is endemic to multiculturalism. It is, in fact, endemic to value-pluralism in all its forms. Belief in value-pluralism is the view that many different activities and forms of life are valuable ... The plurality and mutual exclusivity of valuable activities and forms and styles of life is a commonplace. It becomes philosophically significant the moment one rejects a still pervasive belief in the reducibility of all values to one value which serves as a common denominator to the multiplicity of valuable ways of life ... Value-pluralism is the doctrine which denies that such a reduction is possible. It takes the plurality of valuable activities and ways of life to be ultimate and ineliminable.[11]

Raz goes on to note that a tension is ineliminable from value-pluralism:

Tension is an inevitable concomitant of accepting the truth of value-pluralism. And it is a tension without stability, without a resting point of reconciliation of the two perspectives, the one recognizing the validity of competing values and the one hostile to them.[12]

Stated in Berlinian terms, Raz's point is that when rivalrous values are embodied in mutually exclusive cultures, their incompatibility cannot be other than agonistic. The relations of cultures constituted by uncombinable values will be competitive, even when their formal relationship is one of peaceful coexistence. When they share, or overlap, the same territory, their relations will often be ones of enmity. There is – on Berlin's view, as on Raz's – no way of avoiding these possibilities of tragic conflict, which arise from the embodiment of conflicting values in mutually exclusive ways of life. A world containing such diverse ways of life is far richer in values than a world of cosmopolitans, but it also contains tragic conflicts that a wholly cosmopolitan world would lack. That this could not be otherwise is a further evidence, if one were needed, in support of the truth of value-pluralism.

The most tragic aspect of the conflict of ways of life arises from the fact that membership of forms of cultural life can never be entirely voluntary and is typically unchosen. It is the experience of particularistic identity as an unchosen fate, and the reassertion of ancestral identity against the pressures for its disappearance through assimilation into a larger culture, that are central elements in Berlin's own life-long commitment to the project of a Jewish national home-land, to Zionism. Stuart Hampshire has illuminatingly characterized Berlin's Zionism when he writes:

> Within a political philosophy that recognizes and encour-ages a plurality of ways of life and a plurality of moral values, each with their distinct history, Zionism is still a special case. It cannot be understood simply as a form of nationalism, because the Zionist programme was to create a nation from scattered elements, having very different forms of life and different languages, elements held together only by the vestiges of a shared and peculiar religion. The idea of the nation had to be constructed on the basis, first, of a shared inheritance of religious observancy, and secondly, of a shared history of per-secution.[13]

As Hampshire himself goes on to observe, Zionism was itself, originally and in part, a reactive phenomenon,

> . . . a side-effect of the agitation of ultra-nationalist par-ties and groups in Europe, particularly as this agitation was associated with pogroms in Russia and with anti-Semitic movements elsewhere, as in Vienna around the turn of the century and in France during *l'affaire Dreyfus* . . . the plan for a national home for Jews in Palestine was a natural and rational response to persisting anti-Semitism.[14]

It is worth adding that Zionism – at any rate its expression in the successful foundation of the state of Israel – was, also, a natural and rational response to the immeasurable moral horror of the Holocaust.

Three points are worth making about Berlin's Zionism, specifically, as it fits into the broader liberal framework of his thought. The first is its clear coherence with his liberal version of particularism – his insight that individual well-being demands common cultural forms, and that individual self-identity and self-esteem require the respectful recognition of these cultural forms by others. Further, Berlin's Zionism is fully consonant with his conviction that the political embodiment of these common cultural forms in a sovereign state is a natural human demand, especially in the historical context of the modern world, in which the nation-state is the pre-eminent political form, and in which the people which is the bearer of common forms of cultural life has been subject – as the Jewish people has been subject – to millennial persecution. It is not, indeed, that Berlin asserts, as a matter of universal principle or doctrine, in the fashion of Wilsonianism, that common cultural forms are everywhere to be embodied in the political institution of sovereign statehood. It is rather that, seeing that the human need for such forms is universal and their varieties immense, and perceiving that the common forms of life of Jews had, virtually everywhere, gone unprotected from persecution, he considers the case for a national Jewish homeland to be a very strong one.

It becomes overwhelming when it is recognized that the alternative – assimilation – is unattainable, and Jewish identity a fate which does not arise from, and cannot be escaped by, any act of choice. As Berlin says, in his important and neglected essay on 'Jewish Slavery and Emancipation':

Large-scale assimilation has not in modern times – whatever may have occurred in earlier ages – proved to be a practicable alternative. The German Jews who believed and practised it with the most sincere conviction have suffered the most tragic fate of all.[15]

Berlin is clear that assimilation is, for Jews, rarely a reliable assurance against persecution. His sensitive and clairvoyantly empathetic account of the lives and personalities of Benjamin Disraeli and Karl Marx[16] not only illustrates his belief in the importance of cultural membership for individual well-being, in the cases of these socially alienated Jewish intellectuals, it also suggests – if it never states explicitly – that the different strategies of assimilation these two adopted for shedding their Jewish identity were equally futile. His conviction that assimilation is, in general, a delusive project for Jews is evident in his sympathetic account of the beliefs of his friend Chaim Weizmann, of whom he says in his memoir of him:

> Early in life he accepted the proposition that the ills of the Jews were caused principally by the abnormality of their social situation; and that so long as they remained everywhere a semi-helot population, relegated to an inferior and dependent status, which produced in them the virtues and vices of slaves, their neuroses, both individual and collective, were not curable . . . Personal integrity and strength were not enough: unless their social and political position was somehow altered – made normal – brought into line with that of other peoples, the vast majority of Jews would remain permanently liable to become morally and socially crippled, objects of compassion to the kindly, and of deep distaste to the fastidious. For this there was no remedy save a revolution – a total social transformation – a mass emancipation.[17]

It is because Jews in modern times, if not throughout their history of unparalleled persecution, have not had the real option of assimilation, that Berlin considers the case for a Jewish homeland to be unanswerable. It is so, because without it Jews elsewhere can never be safe from persecution, and because it meets the need for political institutions which mirror the cultural identity of a people which Jews possess along with all other human beings. This latter need is to be understood, in the case of the Jewish people, in the context of a history which *is* that of a persecuted people – persecuted to a degree that is perhaps unique in human history. In this sense, even in Berlin's thought, Zionism remains a special case – though an eminently reasonable one, and one that is in no way at odds with the rest of his thought.

A second feature of Berlin's Zionism is that he does not deny, and indeed actively affirms, the justice of many of the claims of the Palestinian citizens of the state of Israel, but sees their reconciliation with those of Israel as inherently difficult, problematic and even tragic. He is as condemnatory of the pathologies of nationalism as they arise in Israel as he is of them anywhere else. Here he is at one with the founders of the Zionist movement who, without denying its particularistic character as an expression of the historic destiny of the Jews, at the same time associated it with the humanistic ideals, and the conception of a universalistic civil society, expressed in the *Aufklärung*. It is as the embodiment of the ideals of its founders, as a state committed to the ideals of the Enlightenment, that Berlin remains a (far from uncritical) supporter of the state of Israel.

A third feature of Berlin's Zionism generates the most fundamental issues of all. It has always been a feature of Judaism that, in all or most of its varieties, it has acknowledged and affirmed the weight and validity of particularistic obligations and allegiances, without ever denying the reality of ethical demands that are generically human and universal. This duality in Judaism haunts the state of Israel today, as it struggles to reconcile its humanist and its particularistic inheritances. It is present in Berlin's thought, particularly as this is an attempt at a reconciliation of the ideals of Enlightenment humanism with the insights – at once voluntaristic and particularistic – of the Romantics. Berlin's value-pluralism, after all, entails the result that there may be, as indeed there is, in historical reality, an irreducible diversity of worthwhile ways of life, each with its own virtues and excellences, and to any of which a reasonable and specific allegiance may be owed. This is a result that undercuts, not only the creed of the Enlightenment, at least in its simplest forms, as we find it in the works of Condorcet and Paine, say, but also all the universalist faiths – Christianity, Islam and Buddhism, for example. The pluralist thesis is a challenge, for this reason, not only to dominant Western traditions, but to a central human tradition. If there is a *philosophia perennis*, it is in the claim that there is a best way of life, one true good, for all human beings. This perennial philosophy Berlin's pluralism undermines. It may not be fanciful to conjecture that, among the many sources of Berlin's master idea of pluralism, there may be that aspect of his own plural inheritance, that aspect of Judaism in which the validity of irreducibly particularistic (and on occasion rivalrous) allegiances is affirmed.

The particularism Berlin espouses invokes a conception of cultural forms – of dress, architecture, the arts, manners, mores and, above all, of languages – as expressions or embodiments, deposits or vehicles, of human identity. They are not, principally or primarily, means to ends, instruments to want-satisfaction or strategies for purposive action, as perhaps classical utilitarianism conceived them to be.[18] Our identities are inextricably bound up in the web of practices, in the culture in which we come to reflective self-awareness, and which reflects or mirrors our identity. We may even, inverting the customary metaphor, follow Hampshire in seeing thought as the shadow of speech,[19] and the interior life as a shadow cast by the common life. Even if we do not go so far, we will, if we follow Berlin in his Herderian expressivism, see that we are not, in our deepest natures, detachable monads, sovereign choice-makers whose cultural inheritance is for them an accidental encumbrance. Indeed, in so far as our identities are supervenient upon common cultural forms, Herderian expressivism may be in tension with Fichtean voluntarism, the view of cultural forms as historic creations, as collective acts of will, both of which are elements in the Romantic reaction against the Enlightenment. This is a tension to which I shall return, when I consider in more systematic detail Berlin's account of the thinkers of the Counter-Enlightenment.

In the Counter-Enlightenment, as Berlin calls it, and in the Romantic movement, particularism was turned into a doctrine of radical will, and into a denial of all generically human and universal standards, which Berlin has never endorsed. It is of the very essence of Berlin's objective pluralism in ethical theory, and of his agonistic liberalism in political thought, that accepting the truths contained in the Romantic critique of the Enlightenment need not, and does not, commit one to accepting the doctrinal excesses of the Counter-Enlightenment, or to denying entirely, as the thinkers of the Counter-Enlightenment did, the rational and moral unity of mankind. It is to the delicate project of reconciling the insights of these troubling thinkers with the commitments of a chastened liberalism that Berlin's whole thought is directed. A central question in Berlin's project of reconciliation is that of specifying the scope and limits of the rational and moral unity of mankind that remains, once all the force of the pluralism, and consequent endorsement of the validity of particularistic allegiances, emphasized by critics of the Enlightenment, has been accepted. A related, and no less profound question concerns the extent to which Berlin can accept the radical voluntarism of the Romantic and Counter-Enlightenment thinkers – their view that the plural and conflicting ends in which cultural and political life abounds are not only discovered as elements in our complex and self-transforming natures, but also created, invented, brought into being by acts of will, individual and collective. This is a central question for Berlin inasmuch as, for all his criticisms of classical and modern rationalism, he remains himself a rationalist,[20] one committed to the project of rendering the natural and human worlds rationally intelligible. The question is whether this project can be squared with the elements of voluntarism he adopts from the Romantic and reactionary critics of the Enlightenment.

It is a question that arises at the very heart of Berlin's thought, since it suggests a question as to how far human nature is subject to wilful self-transformation, how far novel forms of life can be created by acts of will. In so far as these acts of will are collective, rather than primarily individual, as they were for J. G. Fichte, it suggests a fundamental question as to the coherence of Berlin's pluralism with his liberalism – the possibility that, in so far as liberalism constrains the possibilities of collective self-creation, it may be subverted – or at least limited – by the deeper truth of pluralism. Perhaps most fundamentally of all, Berlin's apparent acceptance of the claims of the critics of the Enlightenment he discusses with such illuminating profundity – that not only may conflicts among values be resolved by acts of will rather than by reflective choice-making and must be so resolved when they are conflicts among incommensurables, but that these very values themselves may be expressions of will, not enduring needs of a constant human nature, however minimal – raises the question of whether Berlin's liberal commitment can, on his own account, have any foundation in human nature. Is it the case, as Berlin maintains, that the ground of liberalism, understood as a commitment to freedom, is the human propensity to choice-making, itself conceived to be universal? Is the privileged status and value of choice-making as a human activity derivable from the universal reality of conflict and incommensurability among values? Or is liberalism itself an act of commitment to a particular way of life that – by the logic of Berlin's own value-pluralism – can claim no universal authority?

It is this last possibility, that values animating entire forms of life may not be grounded in even the complex and contradictory needs of an enduring human nature, that is suggested by J. G. Hamann, and articulated by his disciple J. G. Herder in his doctrines of populism and expressivism. It is the possibility that ultimate values may be groundless acts of individual and collective will, which Berlin himself has called the apotheosis of the Romantic will.[21] This is the species of voluntarist irrationalism, espoused by Kierke-gaard and by Schopenhauer, later restated by Nietzsche and by (at any rate the earlier) Heidegger, but whose fountain-head is the thought of Hamann, that inspires all the varieties of modern irrationalism that come together in what Berlin terms the Counter-Enlightenment.

5 Romanticism and the Counter-Enlightenment

For Voltaire, Diderot, Helvétius, Holbach, Condorcet, there is only one universal civilization, of which now one nation, now another, represents the richest flowering. For Herder there is a plurality of incommensurable cultures. To belong to a given community, to be connected with its members by indissoluble and impalpable ties of a common language, historical memory, habit, tradition and feeling, is a basic human need no less natural than that for food or drink or security or procreation. One nation can understand and sympathize with the institutions of another only because it knows how much its own mean to itself. Cosmopolitanism is the shedding of all that makes one most human, most oneself.

Isaiah Berlin, 'The Counter-Enlightenment'[1]

The *philosophes* proposed to rationalize communication, by inventing a universal language free from the irrational survivals, the idiosyncratic twists and turns, the capricious peculiarities of existing tongues; if they were to succeed, this would be disastrous, for it is precisely the individual historical development of a language that belongs to a people that absorbs, enshrines, and encapsulates a vast wealth of half-conscious, half-remembered collective experience. What men call superstition and prejudice are but the crust of custom which by sheer survival has shown itself proof against the ravages and vicissitudes of its long life; to lose it is to lose the shield that protects men's national existence, their spirit, the habits, memories, faith that have made them what they are. The conception of human nature which the radical critics have promulgated and on which their whole house of cards rests is an infantile fantasy.

Rousseau asks why it is that man, who was born free, is nevertheless everywhere in chains; one might as well ask, says Maistre, why it is that sheep, who are born carnivorous, nevertheless everywhere nibble grass. Men are not born for freedom, nor for peace.

Isaiah Berlin, 'The Counter-Enlightenment'[2]

One is not committed to applauding or even condoning the extravagances of romantic irrationalism if one concedes that, by revealing that the ends of men are many, often unpredictable, and some among them incompatible with one another, the romantics have dealt a fatal blow to the proposition that, all appearances to the contrary, a definite solution of the jigsaw puzzle is, at least in principle, possible, that power in the service of reason can achieve it, that rational organization can bring about the perfect union of such values and counter-values as individual liberty and social equality, spontaneous expression and organized socially dictated efficiency, perfect knowledge and perfect happiness, the claims of personal life and the claims of parties, classes, nations, the public interest. If some ends recognized as fully human are at the same time ultimate and mutually incompatible, then the idea of a golden age, a perfect society compounded of a synthesis of all the correct solutions to all the central problems of human life, is shown to be incoherent in principle. This is the service rendered by romanticism and in particular the doctrine that forms its heart, namely, that morality is moulded by the will and that ends are created, not discovered.'

Isaiah Berlin, 'The Apotheosis of the Romantic Will'[3]

The Counter-Enlightenment is coeval with the Enlightenment itself. There is a legitimate question, to be sure, as to when the Enlightenment began as an intellectual movement, just as there are decisive differences between the Enlightenment that occurred in France, and those which manifested themselves in Germany and Scotland. It is in France that the Enlightenment assumed its central and paradigmatic form, however, and, though it would be incongruous to term him a thinker of the Enlightenment, it is in René Descartes that the most fundamental project of the Enlightenment, that of purging the human mind of all that is irrational, doubtful or groundless, and of reconstituting human thought and practice on rational foundations, is initiated. It is accordingly in Descartes that the first and most formidable critics of Enlightenment rationalism, Pascal and Vico, see their principal opponent. This is so, inasmuch as Vico sees in Descartes, with his method of systematic doubt and of clear and distinct ideas, the chief enemy of his *nuova scienza*, no less than did Pascal, with his distinction between *l'esprit de geometrie* and *l'esprit de finesse*. To be sure, before anything can be discerned of the Enlightenment as an intellectual movement, there were sceptics, Pyrrhonists – latter-day disciples of the ancient Greek sceptic Pyrrho – such as Montaigne, Charron, La Mothe le Vayer, Bayle, who sought (and in considerable measure achieved) the humiliation of human reason, much as the ancient sceptical thinkers, such as Sextus Empiricus and Pyrrho himself, had done, with the difference that these later thinkers did so, by their own account, in the service of the Christian faith. These French Pyrrhonists were precursors of the critics of the Enlightenment because they preceded the Enlightenment, whereas in Vico and Pascal we find a statement of enmity, a declaration of war on René Descartes and his system of thought, on that Cartesian method which had itself had a profound animating influence on all the *philosophes*, even when they rejected it for the sake of empiricism.

It is only with Joseph de Maistre, born in Savoy in 1753, that there arises in France a radical reaction to the Enlightenment, one which Berlin tells us is more penetrating than that of J. J. Rousseau,[4] inasmuch as Rousseau retained the Enlightenment beliefs in natural man, in human goodness, and in a social contract, which de Maistre set out to destroy. Rousseau retained, also, the belief in the final compatibility of human ends – the belief that there existed, or could be imagined, a form of human society in which all genuine human needs were met, even if the historical record was one of movement away from this ideal rather than of progress towards it – a belief which the most powerful and challenging critics of the Enlightenment, who were not French but German, sought to shatter. It is Herder, Fichte, and, perhaps above all, J. G. Hamann, that Berlin sees as the principal exponents of the Counter-Enlightenment, the spiritual fathers of that modern irrationalism that has torn up by its roots the living structure of thought that was once the Enlightenment, and which has infused our civilization with the idea of radical will that is central to Romanticism.

If he affirms that the greatest critics of the Enlightenment were German, not French, this is not to say that Berlin belittles Maistre. On the contrary, he sees in Maistre one of the most subtle and merciless critics of Enlightenment humanism and rationalism. For Berlin, Maistre is a thinker whose insights into the character of language as the embodiment of unconscious historical memory make those of Edmund Burke seem superficial and Whiggish, and whose grasp of the peaceless ferocity of the human animal, and its capacity for and disposition towards self-immolation, renders Hobbes's account of man tame and bland. (It is worth noting in parenthesis that, for all his vaunted realism, Hobbes is in Berlin's terms a monist and a rationalist – and a pretty simple-minded one at that.)[5] When Maistre tells us that he has made the acquaintance of Frenchmen and Englishmen, Italians and Spaniards, but never of man,[6] he states pithily the objection to the Enlightenment conception of abstract universal humanity that is later developed by Herder. When he represents reason and analysis as corrosive and destructive, solvents of custom and allegiance that cannot replace the bonds of sentiment and tradition which they weaken or demolish, he illuminates, better perhaps than any subsequent writer, the absurdity of the Enlightenment faith (for such it undoubtedly was) that human society can have a rational foundation. If to reason is to question, then questioning will have no end, until it has wrought the dissolution of the civilization that gave it birth.

When Maistre portrays Nature, not as the benign matron of the *philosophes*, but as wasteful, pitiless, predatory and murderous, he gives us a critique of Enlightenment naturalism that is unsurpassed, echoed in its intensity only in the eccentric and long neglected writings of de Sade. And, in a related critique, when he portrays savage mankind, not as the hospitable primitives of the imaginary travellers of the Encyclopedia, but as 'cruel, dissolute and brutal',[7] he undermines one of the central myths of the Enlightenment, that the corruptions of civilization are somehow unnatural, rather than being merely another expression of the natural human savagery which he finds in the pre-civilized human condition. Like Dostoevsky, with whom he has a good deal in common, Maistre portrays man as a pitiful creature, riddled with desperate and incorrigible contradictions:

> He does not know what he wants; he wants what he does not want; he does not want what he wants; he *wants to want*; he sees within himself something which is not himself, and which is stronger than himself. The wise man resists and cries *'Who will deliver me?'* The fool gives in and calls his weakness happiness.[8]

Maistre's account of man the 'monstrous centaur'[9] has far more in common with Dostoevsky's Grand Inquisitor than it does with Augustine, with Bossuet or Bonald, because, like Dostoevsky and unlike these reactionary traditionalists, he is our contemporary in the depth and profundity of his irrationalist conviction of the fragility of civilized order. Notwithstanding his backward-looking and, to us, irrelevant ultramontanism (his belief that the Church should possess political as well as spiritual authority) he is a far starker modernist than the more moderate Burke, or than most, if not all, of his Enlightenment enemies. He is in truth as Berlin summarizes him:

> To his contemporaries, perhaps to himself, he seemed to be gazing calmly into the classical and feudal past, but what he saw even more clearly proved to be a blood-freezing vision of the future.[10]

It is nevertheless among the Germans that Berlin finds the central thinkers of Romanticism and the Counter-Enlightenment, most seminal among them J. G. Hamann. This thinker, as profound and as neglected by his contemporaries as was Vico, but having among his disciples one of the fathers of modern irrationalism, Sören Kierkegaard, was heir to a native German tradition of mystical reflection that included Jacob Boehme, Meister Eckhart, Angelus Silesius and many others. These pietistic and devotional writers combined a conviction of the ineffability of spiritual truth with a view of language, later adopted and developed by Herder, as the pervasive structure of human thought and activity. For them language was not a neutral medium of communication, but a store-house of memories and truths not accessible to critical human awareness, yet preserved in language and used by human beings in all their activities and interactions. It was Herder who developed Hamann's scattered insights about language into a more or less systematic critique of the 'designative model'[11] of language-use that had dominated thought about it at least since Hobbes, Bacon and Locke and their English empiricist successors, and which had been given a naïvely systematic articulation by Condillac in France. In this model the primitive units of meaning are *names*, and the primordial activity of language is the representation or signifying of a reality that is not itself linguistic. Language is then an ancillary to human thought and activity, its amanuensis, not its master. For Hamann, as for Herder, this view of language, as of human activity in general, is a complete mistake. As Berlin puts it, paraphrasing Vico's anticipation of their view:

> A utilitarian interpretation of the most essential human activities is misleading. They are, in the first place, purely expressive; to sing, to dance, to worship, to fight, and the institutions which embody these activities, comprise a vision of the world. Language, religious rites, myths, laws, social, religious, judicial institutions, are forms of self-expression, of wishing to convey what one is and strives for; they obey intelligible patterns, and for that reason it is possible to reconstruct the life of other societies, even those remote in time and place and utterly primitive, by asking what kind of framework of human ideas, acts, could have generated the poetry, the movements, the mythology which was their natural expression.[12]

Again, in his recently published study of Hamann, Berlin characterizes Hamann's view of language as follows:

> 'Language is the first and last organ and criterion of reason', said Hamann. The Cartesian notion that there are ideas, clear and distinct, which can be contemplated by a kind of inner eye, a notion common to all the rationalists, and peddled in its empirical form by Locke and his followers – ideas in their pure state, unconnected with words and capable of being translated into any of them indifferently – that is the central fallacy that for him needed eliminating. The facts were otherwise. Language is what we think with, not translate into: the meaning of the notion of 'language' is symbol-using.[13]

Berlin expands on Hamann's conception of language:

> For Hamann thought and language are one . . . Because this is so, philosophy, which pretends to be the critique of things, or at best ideas about them, since it is nothing

but words about words – second-order judgements – is in fact a critique of our use of language or symbols. If it had been the case that there was a metaphysical structure of things which could somehow be directly perceived, or if there were a guarantee that our ideas, or even our linguistic usage, in some mysterious way corresponded to such an objective structure, it might be supposed that philosophy, either by direct metaphysical intuition, or by attending to ideas or to language ... was a method of knowing and judging reality. But for Hamann this is a thoroughly fallacious conception, though time-honoured – indeed one on which the whole of European rationalism has been built. The notion of a correspondence, that there is an objective world on one side, and, on the other, man and his instruments – language, ideas and so forth – attempting to approximate to this objective reality, is a false picture.[14]

There are several component elements in Hamann's conception of language, itself seen by him as paradigmatic of all the most important human activities, which were developed by Herder, and which are worth remarking upon. One has already been introduced – the thesis that the role of language is not instrumental or strategic, but constitutive and expressive, in respect of human beings and their cultures. The second is perhaps less familiar, but no less important. This is that language is not a set of words, of names, a constellation of linguistic atoms or modular units of meaning, which can be assembled and disassembled at will, but a network, which is linked together at every point. This linguistic or semantic *holism*, the idea of a language such that to use it at any point is to invoke, to touch or be touched by, all the rest, is only an instance or application of an idea that is perhaps not much older than Hamann and Herder, the idea of a *culture* – the idea, that is to say, of a people as having a pervasive form of life, in terms of which their activities, however otherwise disparate or miscellaneous, are given coherence and are renewed over time. A culture, like a language, is not an amalgam, an album of singularities, a collection of random sweepings; it expresses and is animated by a set of ideas or values that is distinctive and even peculiar to it, and by which it is for that reason properly individuated and recognized.

This holism about language and about culture is integral to the *expressivism* which is defended both by Hamann and by Herder. It underpins the critique that the expressivist conception of human activity incorporates of the Enlightenment anthropology, and of the uses to which that anthropology was put in moral and political thought of the Enlightenment, as that is found in utilitarian and contractarian philosophies alike. Both for classical utilitarianism, and for theorists of the social contract such as Hobbes, Locke, and Rousseau, it makes sense to employ a 'resolutive-compositive method' in respect of human society, to break it down into modular units, whereby to reassemble it by acts of calculation or agreement. For Hamann and Herder, as for Maistre, such disaggregation is an impossibility, or else wholly destructive, in virtue of the character of cultural forms as living wholes, not summations or aggregations of atomistic elements. Following Wittgenstein, a later exponent of this same view,[15] we may say that human society cannot be constituted by agreement or calculation, since both are themselves forms of social life, presuppositions and not foundations of human intercourse. To suppose that society could be created by agreement is to neglect the fact that agreement, like language, is a form of social life. Agreement follows on social life; it cannot found it. As Berlin states Hamann's view: '. . . the existence of a complex web of human relations was presupposed by the very possibility of human thought, and did not need its products as its justification.'[16]

A third idea of Hamann and Herder about language is that of the particularity of natural languages and forms of cultural life. No one is born speaking Esperanto, and the ideal of a universal language, however primordial it may itself be, is just that, an ideal, that is to say, a creature of the human imagination. The universal reality is that of the diversity of tongues. Languages, like cultures, are individuated by what they disallow, prohibit and exclude, as much as by what they prescribe. They are at one, most unequivocally, in their differences from one another. One may even say that the diversity of natural languages is no accident. It expresses a deeper diversity, that in human natures, or forms of human life, itself expressive of the indeterminacy introduced in the species by its common capacity for choice-making, and so for self-creation. The diversity of natural languages and what it embodies, the diversity of forms of common life among human beings, exemplifies the necessary diversity of human identities, that they are not merely plural, but different, exclusive, constituted by their very differences. This is the application to whole ways of life of the pluralist thesis about specific goods or values – that they are sometimes constitutively uncombinable. In respect of forms of common life this pluralist thesis implies not only difference, but the constitutive or necessary difference of mutual exclusivity. The virtues of the great-souled man and of the Christian saint cannot coexist in the same person, and they cannot be fully realized in the same culture. In their very natures they are bound to exclude one another. It is a distinctive feature of languages, then, that they be not only diverse or plural, but that they also be particular and individuated by their differences from one another, even as cultures are. It is these aspects of language and culture, subversive of the universalist or uniformitarian anthropology of the Enlightenment, that Berlin finds among the Romantics, and that are consilient with his own pluralism.

There is in the Romantic thinkers another set of ideas, not obviously of a piece with the ideas of expressivism and holism in language and culture sketched above, which are ideas about novelty and individuality, and their relations with will, that are also echoed in Berlin's thought. Central to the Western tradition that derives from the Greeks is the idea of art as craftsmanship, as the embodiment of an eternal, timeless prototype, as a form of *anamnesis* or recollection, even as knowledge itself is remembering and ignorance forgetting. On such a view there can indeed be nothing that is new under the sun. A very different conception inspires Jewish and Christian traditions, that of the idea of creation, even *ex nihilo*, and it is this idea, substantially secularized, that the Romantics invoked when they attached supreme value to creativity in art and life. To them, creativity certainly could never be expressed in the application of a rule or obedience to a tradition; it was most likely to be found in rebellion against rules and forms that are external, unauthentic, merely technical or calculational. This is one of the roots in Romanticism of contemporary irrationalism.

Here again Hamann's thought is exemplary. Hamann had lauded Hume for his dissolution of natural causation, for demonstrating that scepticism or questioning ended in the extinction of activity, not in Cartesian certainty, for showing by reason that all things are possible, that we live by faith alone, by *Glaube*,[17] not by rational reflection or deliberation. In Hamann, Hume's Pyrrhonist critique of human reason is invoked in support of a radical fideism that later, in less pietistic thinkers, became a doctrine of the creative efficacy of the human will, or, in Schopenhauer, a metaphysical affirmation of the primacy of universal will.

Among the Romantics, the apotheosis of will took the form of an elevation of the particular over the general, an assertion that what individuated peoples or cultures or works of art was not their membership of any genus or the exemplification of any type, but rather what was peculiar or unique to them. We have here a form of the doctrine of mystical silence, or ineffability, as that was developed, through a long line of mystical German thinkers from Eckhart to Mauthner and the early Wittgenstein – the form in which it is (as Goethe famously put it)[18] the individual that is ineffable. It is not far from this view to the view, found in many twentieth-century irrationalists such as D. H. Lawrence, that thought kills, that abstraction maims and reflection paralyses vitality, in individuals as well as in peoples.

These ideas of the Romantic Counter-Enlightenment were evoked, in part, by elements of the Enlightenment itself: they were episodes in the self-undermining of the Enlightenment that occurred as an unintended result of the efforts of its greatest thinkers. It is an irony of intellectual history that the theory of the will to power of Nietzsche, the irrationalism of Sorel, the exaltation of the unconscious and of the pre-linguistic in Surrealism and Expressionism, the cult of energy and of the triumph of the will in inter-war fascism, as that is expressed in the poetry of D'Annunzio and the writings of Junger, are all prefigured in the Romantics' destructive critique of rational analysis, their insistent declaration of the impotence and servility of human reason in comparison with the power of instinct and will; and that in all this their inspiration was, in part, the Kantian ideal of the autonomy of the human will. The jargon of authenticity, as that is found in Heidegger and Sartre, is a residue of Romanticism, captured in an idiom derived proximately from Husserl, but ultimately from Kierkegaard, himself Hamann's boldest and most gifted follower. In Kierkegaard, the impact of Hamann's irrationalism was to make not only diverse ethical values incommensurable by reason, but the different spheres of life – ethical, aesthetic, religious – themselves incommensurable. It was left to Kierkegaard, and in another, neo-pagan idiom, to Nietzsche, to consummate the dissolution of reason which Hamann's work, and the Romantic movement, had inaugurated.

The irony is that, even as Hamann's irrationalist fideism was paradoxically strengthened by the infusion of Hume's Pyrrhonism, so the Romantic affirmation of the creativity of the human will was fed by the conception of autonomy bequeathed to German and European thought by the arch-rationalist, Kant. Both these supreme exemplars of the

Enlightenment, Hume and Kant, accordingly, contributed unwittingly to its undoing by the Romantic movement. It is thus that, according to Berlin, the German Counter-Enlightenment received one of its greatest stimuli in Hamann's reception and absorption of the sceptical theorizing of the greatest representative of the Scottish Enlightenment, David Hume. In Hamann the Enlightenment commitments to the constancy of human nature, and to the uniformity of nature itself, which persisted in Hume in the form of a naturalistic epistemology of belief, were done away with, in the service of a mystical affirmation of the unique, and of a revelation that was conceived to be ineffable. In Hamann, too, the empiricist designative view of language was abandoned in favour of a species of semantic holism, of language as a network of inextricably interlinked meanings, that coexisted ambiguously with an ultra-nominalist doctrine of mystical silence – the doctrine that the particularities that make up the world elude language and are ineffable. In all of these doctrinal shifts, however, the empiricist and rationalist elements in Hume's thought, in virtue of which it belongs authentically to an Enlightenment intellectual tradition, drop away. Similarly, in the Romantic appropriation of Kant what was retained was the idea of the autonomy of the human will and the unknowability of things in themselves, while what was dropped was Kantian rationalism. We see in the thought of Schopenhauer the contribution of Kantian philosophy – itself one of the highest points of the European Enlightenment – to the genesis of modern irrationalism.

The importance of the Romantics for Berlin is that, unlike Maistre, who developed a wholly reactive and indeed reactionary critique of the Enlightenment, they developed a systematic alternative to Enlightenment conceptions that was to prove far more influential and enduring than merely defensive responses to them. Again, unlike other, more purely defensive theorists of the Counter-Enlightenment, the Romantics anticipated the most radical and distinctive trends of thought in the late nineteenth and twentieth centuries. The radical voluntarism, accordingly, of the Counter-Enlightenment, the exaltation of creative will over reason, was no merely reactive or defensive phenomenon, but rather an intellectual movement of genuine power and insight, whose vitality derived in part from its exploitation of self-undermining aspects of the Enlightenment itself.

It is no less clear that Berlin finds the doctrinal excesses of the Counter-Enlightenment, as they are made clear in the later thought of Fichte, for example, wholly unacceptable. The key Romantic idea and value of originality, in art and in life, is accepted by Berlin as a healthy corrective to the uniformitarian rationalism of the Enlightenment, and a necessary response to the limits of human reason when it is confronted by undecidable dilemmas in practice. This Romantic idea may even be found to be restated by Berlin himself, when he affirms that there are meaningful questions without any one true answer, when he echoes the Romantics in denying that evil and falsehood are many but truth and goodness one, when he affirms that in a clash of values, commitments, allegiances or forms of life that are incommensurable, our only recourse can be to a decision that is itself groundless – in short, to an act of will. In these and related respects, Berlin's own thought endorses the principal thesis, not indeed of Maistre's reactionary critique of the Enlightenment, but of the Romantic Counter-Enlightenment.

The celebration of singularity in human life, of all that which is surd and not merely the exemplar of a valuable type, the claim that, when incommensurable values and counter-values must be reconciled in practice, it is human commitment and authenticity rather than reflective deliberation, or reason, that are called upon – these are themes that are common to the Romantic critics of the Enlightenment and to Berlin. In the post-Romantic period these ideas were invoked to justify wild excesses in theory and practice, to license a particularism of nations or races that had been liberated from all common or universal standards, and to subvert altogether the Enlightenment idea of the moral and intellectual unity of the species. The post-Romantic legacy of particularism and voluntarism was a demolition of that common framework of categories of thought which, together with the capacity for self-creation through choice-making, Berlin advances as the surviving form of a common human nature. In this post-Romantic phase of European thought, the very idea of objective standards, however plural, that constrain individual or collective will, is relinquished, and along with it the idea of the worlds of fact and value as independent subject-matters, neither wholly constituted by, nor entirely alterable by, human will. In this post-Romantic period, not only the Enlightenment, but the intellectual inheritance of Europe seems to have suffered a caesura, such that its unity has been irreparably broken. The legacy of the Romantics, then, has been to shatter not only the Enlightenment but also the classical inheritance of European culture.

The question that arises for Berlin's system of ideas is whether his doctrines of objective pluralism and of agonistic liberalism, as I have termed them, permit him to retain key Enlightenment commitments to human emancipation, to liberty and to cross-cultural communication and evaluation, while accepting the Romantic and Counter-Enlightenment claims as to the incommensurability of cultures and the role of the will in individual and collective self-creation. Of Berlin's endorsement of central aspects of the Enlightenment project there can be no reasonable doubt: as he puts his view of the Enlightenment, canonically, in his study of Hamann:

> ... there were certain beliefs that were more or less common to the entire party of progress and civilization, and this is what makes it proper to speak of it as a single movement. These were, in effect, the conviction that the world, or nature, was a single whole, subject to a single

set of laws, in principle discoverable by the intelligence of man; that the laws which governed inanimate nature were in principle the same as those which governed plants, animals and sentient beings; that man was capable of improvement; that there existed certain objectively recognizable human goals which all men, rightly so described, sought after, namely, happiness, knowledge, justice, liberty, and what was somewhat vaguely described but well understood as virtue; that these goals were common to all men as such, were not unattainable, nor incompatible, and that human misery, vice and folly were mainly due to ignorance either of what these goals consisted in or of the means of attaining them – ignorance due in turn to insufficient knowledge of the laws of nature . . . Consequently, the discovery of general laws that govern human behaviour, their clear and logical integration into scientific systems – of psychology, sociology, economics, political science and the like (though they did not use these names) – and the determination of their proper place in the great corpus of knowledge that covered all discoverable facts, would, by replacing the chaotic amalgam of guesswork, tradition, superstition, prejudice, dogma, fantasy and 'interested error' that hitherto did service as human knowledge and human wisdom (and of which by far the chief protector and instigator was the Church), create a new, sane, rational, happy, just and self-perpetuating human society, which, having arrived at the peak of attainable perfection, would preserve itself against all hostile influences, save perhaps those of nature.[19]

Berlin gives an equally canonical assessment of the central beliefs of the Enlightenment, and of their effects in practice, when he writes:

A very great deal of good, undoubtedly, was done, suffering mitigated, injustice avoided or prevented, ignorance exposed, by the conscientious attempt to apply scientific methods to the regulation of human affairs ... But the central dream, the demonstration that everything in the world moved by mechanical means, that all evils could be cured by technological steps, that there could exist engineers both of human souls and of human bodies, proved delusive. Nevertheless, it proved less misleading in the end than the attacks upon it in the nineteenth century by means of arguments equally fallacious, but with implications that were, both intellectually and politically, more sinister and oppressive. The intellectual power, honesty, lucidity, courage, and disinterested love of the most gifted thinkers of the eighteenth century remain to this day without parallel. Their age is one of the best and most hopeful episodes in the life of mankind.[20]

As against this strongly positive assessment of the Enlightenment, Berlin has also said in favour of the Romantic Counter-Enlightenment that 'this at least may be set to its credit: that it has permanently shaken the faith in universal, objective truth in matters of conduct, in the possibility of a perfect and harmonious society, wholly free from conflict or injustice or oppression – a goal for which no sacrifice can be too great if men are ever to create Condorcet's reign of truth, happiness and virtue, bound "by an indissoluble chain" – an ideal for which more human beings have, in our time, sacrificed themselves and others than, perhaps, for any other cause in human history.'[21] In this statement the illusory Enlightenment ideal of a harmonious society is identified as one – perhaps the greatest – source of war and tyranny in our time.

The question for Berlin is how his endorsement of the Enlightenment project, however highly qualified, can cohere with the ideas he has adopted – with whatever deep reservations – from the Romantic Counter-Enlightenment. The differences between Berlin's outlook, arising from his debts to the Romantic thinkers, and that of the Enlightenment, in all its varieties, can perhaps be summarized under three heads. There is first of all the role of reason in Berlin's account of moral and political life, which is far more restricted than any Enlightenment thinker – with the possible exception of Hume – could accept. For Berlin, practical life, moral and political life, abounds in dilemmas that are rationally undecidable, such that, whereas Berlin does not deny the possibility and the reality of moral reasoning, he does reject the Enlightenment project of a fully rational morality. Secondly, because Berlin believes that rationally undecidable dilemmas arising from conflicts among incommensurables are an ineradicable and permanent feature of the human condition, he is bound to reject the Whiggish view of the indefinite improvability of the human circumstance accepted by virtually all the Enlightenment thinkers, with the significant exception, again, of Hume. This does not, of course, mean that he denies that there can be real improvement in the human lot, since his recognition that there are generically human evils, and his affirmation that these can be alleviated to a significant extent, show him acknowledging the possibility of such improvement, and, indeed, in the passages quoted above, advancing the historical thesis that the Enlightenment has itself had a benign influence in this regard. The fact remains that on Berlin's view of the permanence of tragic conflict among incommensurable goods and evils the horizons of possible improvement in human affairs are far narrower than would be allowed by almost all Enlightenment thinkers. This leads to his third difference with the Enlightenment, which is that arising from his repudiation of the Enlightenment ideal of a universal civilization. It is a cardinal element in Berlin's outlook that, without ever endorsing relativism, he rejects the idea of universal convergence on a single form of social life which supported, and gave content to, the Enlightenment idea of civilization. In this he differs even from Hume, for whom history was an alternation of progress with barbarism, and sides with Herder, for whom it was an exfoliation of incommensurable cultures. Berlin, accordingly, rejects the philosophy of history upheld by even the most sceptical of the Enlightenment thinkers. In short, he severely qualifies the rationalism and the meliorism of the Enlightenment *philosophes*, and seems to repudiate altogether the idea of convergence on a universal civilization which is the foundation of the Enlightenment philosophy of history.

There may be a paradox in Berlin's account of the Enlightenment and of the Romantic Counter-Enlightenment yet deeper than those that have been illuminated so far. For, while associating the Enlightenment with the monist doctrines that have animated much modern totalitarian thought and practice, Berlin has at the same time discerned in the pluralistic affirmation of incommensurable values made by the Romantic critics of the Enlightenment a major source of modern conceptions of toleration. He seems to find in the Enlightenment's illiberal Romantic critics a stronger support for liberal ideals than any that can be found in the liberal Enlightenment. If this is so, it is an irony of intellectual history as extraordinary as those to which Berlin has himself explicitly drawn our attention.

The question remains: what supports Berlin's liberalism, given his comprehensive qualification or abandonment of the Enlightenment's central conceptions and his qualified endorsement of some of the chief claims of the Romantic Counter-Enlightenment? What are the prospects for a liberalism, such as Berlin's appears to be, that is, at least in several important respects, post-Enlightenment in its fundamental premises? Or, to put the same question in slightly different terms, the issue arises whether, or how far, the moral and political project of the Enlightenment can survive, when it has been rendered foundationless by the abandonment or destruction of its sustaining philosophical anthropology and of the interpretation of history which that conception of man supports.

6 Agonistic Liberalism

Joseph de Maistre once observed that, when Rousseau asked why it was that men who were born free were nevertheless everywhere in chains, this was like asking why it was that sheep, who were born carnivorous, nevertheless everywhere nibbled grass. Similarly the Russian radical Alexander Herzen observed that we classify creatures by zoological types, according to the characteristics and habits that are most frequently to be found conjoined. Thus, one of the defining attributes of fish is their liability to live in water, hence, despite the existence of flying fish, we do not say of fish in general that their nature or essence – the 'true' end for which they were created – is to fly, since most fish fail to achieve this and do not display the slightest tendency in this direction. Yet in the case of men, and men alone, we say that the nature of man is to seek freedom, even though very few men in the long life of our race have in fact pursued it, and seem contented to be ruled by others, seeking to be well-governed by those who provide them with sufficient food, shelter, rules of life, but not to be self-governed. Why should man alone, Herzen asked, be classified in terms of what at most small minorities here and there have ever sought for its own sake, still less actively fought for? This sceptical reflection was offered by a man whose entire life was dominated by a single-minded passion – the pursuit of liberty, personal and political, of his own and other nations, to which he sacrificed his public career and private happiness.

Isaiah Berlin, *Four Essays on Liberty*[1]

That we cannot have everything is a necessary, not a contingent truth . . . It may be that the ideal of freedom to choose ends without claiming eternal validity for them, and the pluralism of values connected with this, is only the

late fruit of our declining capitalist civilization: an ideal
which remote ages and primitive society have not
recognized, and one which posterity will regard with
curiosity, even sympathy, but little comprehension. This
may be so; but no sceptical conclusions seem to me to
follow. . . . Indeed, the very desire for guarantees that our
values are eternal and secure in some objective heaven is
perhaps only a craving for the certainties of childhood or
the absolute values of our primitive past. 'To realize the
relative validity of our convictions,' said an admirable writer
of our time, 'and yet stand for them unflinchingly, is what
distinguishes a civilized man from a barbarian.' To demand
more than this is perhaps a deep and incurable metaphysical
need; but to allow it to determine one's practice is a
symptom of an equally deep, and more dangerous, moral
and political immaturity.

Isaiah Berlin, Four Essays on Liberty[2]

Berlin's master-thesis of value-pluralism, which is the thesis
of the incommensurability, or incomparability by reason, of
rivalrous goods and evils and forms of life, has the role in
his thought of privileging choice-making as the embodiment
of human self-creation. We make ourselves what we are –
always, it is true, in circumstances that are not of our
making – through our choices. We can do this, because –
unlike the natures of members of other animal species with
which we are familiar – our natures are not fixed or finished;
they are inherently incomplete, liable to self-transformation
by the choices we make among the incommensurable goods
and evils we confront unavoidably in our lives. If our natures
have themselves an element of indeterminacy in them, such
that no one form of life, or even any extended family of
forms of life, and no one hierarchy of goods or excellences,
are their truest expression, then this indeterminacy can be
closed off, provisionally at any rate, only by a groundless
commitment to one among the forms of life with which
we are acquainted, or which suggest themselves to us in

imagination. In the real world in which we find ourselves, there is an irreducible diversity of worthwhile forms of life whose goodness is not commensurable by any universal standard, and within each of which there are goods and evils that are similarly incommensurable. For Berlin, self-creation through choice-making is forced upon us by the uncertainty in our very natures in virtue of which no one form of life is best for us, and by the diversity of rivalrous and incommensurable values we inescapably encounter in our experience.

It is the centrality of choice-making to self-creation, and the necessity of self-creation for creatures such as ourselves, that grounds liberalism in Berlin's thought. But does this argument – the argument from choice-making to freedom, from pluralism to liberalism – succeed? It may be helpful at this stage in our interpretation and assessment of Berlin's work to review in more systematic, explicit and detailed terms the connections that link pluralism with liberalism in his thought. There seem to be three main strands of argument in his writings for this linkage. There is in the first place Berlin's argument for the value of negative liberty – that it is a constitutive component of human self-creation by radical choices among incommensurables. It has value, not merely or even primarily as an aspect of rational autonomy, but as a condition whereby human beings constitute themselves in all the diversity of identities in which they are to be found, now and in human history, including the vast majority in which autonomy does not figure centrally. Negative liberty has value, perhaps (among political goods) pre-eminent value, for Berlin, because it facilitates human self-creation by choice-making among goods and evils that are rationally incomparable. Value-pluralism supports liberalism here in that it is by the choices protected by negative freedom that we negotiate our way among incommensurable values.

This argument has a negative aspect, which may be stated in a way that clarifies the second strand in Berlin's reasoning from pluralism to liberalism. For, if there are goods (and evils) that are rationally incommensurable, then no political authority can have *good reason* to impose any particular combination of them on any of its citizens. Indeed, in so far as different people will be able to embody in their lives combinations of incommensurable goods that are constitutively uncombinable in any single life, there will be good reason for political authority to *refrain from* attempting any such imposition of a pattern of life on its subjects. As Steven Lukes has put this argument, once it has been accepted that there are no 'uniquely determinate solutions rationally compelling upon all', it follows that 'for the state to impose any single solution on some of its citizens is thus (not only from their standpoint) unreasonable.'³ That the state has good reason to refrain from authoritarian intervention in people's lives if value-pluralism is true is also maintained by Bernard Williams, when he argues that 'if there are many and competing genuine values, then the greater the extent to which a society tends to be single-valued, the more genuine values it neglects or suppresses. More, to this extent, must mean better.'⁴ The nub of these arguments is in the claim that if the radical value-pluralist thesis of the rational incomparability of goods and evils is true, then the state can never have sufficient rational justification for imposing any particular ranking of values on people (save that involved in securing the possibility for any sort of worthwhile life). And, because imposing any such ranking would result in the suppression or incomplete realization of some genuine values, the state has good reason *not* to engage in authoritarian or illiberal policies of this kind.

The third strand of argument for the necessary linkage of pluralism with liberalism follows from the second and maintains that the authoritarian denial of freedom presupposes the denial of the truth of value-pluralism. This argument has been well stated by Bernard Williams, when he says that 'the consciousness of the plurality of competing values is itself a good, as constituting knowledge of an absolute and fundamental truth . . . Here Berlin . . . finds value in knowledge and true understanding themselves, and regards it as itself an argument for the liberal society that that society expresses more than any other does a true understanding of the pluralistic nature of values.'[5] Here the argument is once again two-fold: that authoritarian or illiberal societies or regimes are committed necessarily to denying the genuineness or validity of the values they suppress or disfavour; and that liberal societies are ones in which the truth of value-pluralism is accepted and celebrated.

In Berlin's thought, then, the master-thesis of pluralism supports liberalism; but it is a liberalism of a distinctive, and highly original kind. Berlin's liberalism – which is, if I am not mistaken, the most profoundly deliberated, and most powerfully defended, in our time, or, perhaps, in any time – diverges radically from those that have dominated political philosophy in the post-war world, and indeed since J. S. Mill, in many important respects. Its agonistic character, its acknowledgement of an irreducible diversity of rivalrous goods, *including negative and positive liberties*, distinguishes it from all those recent liberalisms that engage themselves in 'theories of justice', or of 'fundamental rights'. *These* liberalisms are destroyed by Berlin's insight that, not only is any sort of liberty only one among many incommensurable values, but the different liberties, negative and positive, are themselves rivalrous and uncombinable and sometimes incommensurable, such that choices must be made among them, without the help of any overarching standard or synoptic theory.

All the dominant liberalisms of our time, whether they be variations on Hobbesian or Lockean, Kantian or Millian themes, have a conception of rational choice at their heart which Berlin's value-pluralism subverts. If I am not mistaken, Berlin's liberalism is by far the most formidable and plausible so far advanced, inasmuch as it acknowledges the limits of rational choice and affirms the reality of radical choice. Whereas all the conventional liberalisms are varieties of moral and political rationalism for which apparently undecidable dilemmas arise from imperfections in our knowledge, understanding or reasoning that are in principle removable, Berlin's liberalism takes its stand on our experience of moral and political life, with all its radical choices. If I am right in my belief that Berlin's is the strongest form of liberal theory we have, then the question whether liberalism is indeed supported by value-pluralism, or whether pluralism is in the end the deeper truth and a truth that undermines liberalism as a political ideal with a universal claim on reason, is no small one. It is the question whether the liberal form of life is ideally the best for all human beings, or is to be regarded as one form of life among many, with no foundation in human nature or the history of the species as a whole. Or, to put the issue at its sharpest, it is the question whether pluralism and liberalism may not be, in general or across a large range of historical circumstances, conflicting and competitive in their implications for practice.

One argument in support of the claim that value-pluralism and liberalism are in no way in tension with one another is made by traditional liberals of both libertarian and egalitarian orientations. For them the pluralist thesis of value-incommensurability is a thesis in axiology, in the theory of value or of the good, and does not bear upon principles of right. This is an argument that has been advanced by latter-day classical liberals[6] and it is one proposed by Kantian liberals such as John Rawls.[7] These liberal thinkers hold that incommensurabilities among values – be they particular goods or whole conceptions of the good – are actually congenial to, and supportive of, liberal principles, since they help to justify liberal conceptions of justice and rights which neither embody nor presuppose any specific conception of the good. In this standard liberal view, principles of justice or liberty are not substantive goods to be traded off against other goods, but regulative principles, principles of right which set the terms on which competing goods and conceptions of the good can be pursued. Liberal principles of justice and liberty are deontic principles which specify constraints on the pursuit of goods; they are in a different category from the goods themselves. Such regulative principles of right will be especially appropriate and necessary, on this view, if value-pluralism is true – if there *are* incommensurable values. For, if the incommensurability thesis is true, then conceptions of maximizing or optimizing what has value, as found in classical utilitarianism, perfectionism and related doctrines, will be inapplicable. On this standard liberal view in which liberal principles are principles of right, then, not only is there no tension between liberalism and value-pluralism, but pluralism is actually congenial to liberalism.

Though cogent and worthy of serious consideration, this common liberal argument does not measure up to the full force of Berlin's value-pluralism (or of the variant of value-pluralism that animates Raz's liberalism). Indeed, this argument presupposes the truth of precisely those conventional liberalisms which Berlin's value-pluralism challenges and that his claim that liberties may embody rivalrous and incommensurable values, if it is at all valid, destroys. The central flaw in this common reasoning is in the assumption that principles of liberty or justice can be insulated from the force of value-incommensurability. If Berlin is on the right track, this is an illusion, since there are conflicting liberties, rival equalities, and incompatible demands of justice. Further, these competing elements in liberal political morality will express values that are sometimes beyond rational comparison. If, as Berlin clearly believes, and as experience plainly suggests, negative liberties do not form a harmonious system but are often incompatible with one another, we will resolve such conflicts only if we attach weights or values to the rival liberties. Sometimes, however, we will have no measure whereby we can give the rival liberties values in a common currency; their values will be incommensurable.

This will be so if the competing liberties under consideration figure significantly in divergent conceptions of the good life, or are embedded in different cultural traditions.

To imagine that liberties cannot compete with one another in their demands on practice is, on the face of it, a fantastic supposition. To suppose that such conflicts, where they occur, can be resolved by appeal to principles which prescribe a unique set of trade-offs among liberties, is to suppose that there can be an entirely deontic political morality. It is to presuppose the possibility of a rights-based liberalism that at no point depends upon controversial conceptions of the good and which never presupposes in its application judgements involving incommensurables. These are all implausibly strong assumptions, and they presuppose that principles of right can be sealed off from conflicts within the good.

This last is a view that both Berlin and Raz, for whom rights gain determinacy only from their contribution to human interests whose contents are themselves complex and variable and which may encompass conflicts that are not rationally arbitrable, are committed to denying. The standard view that liberal principles are regulative principles which can be insulated in their content and application from deep conflicts of values suppresses the fact that the liberties and equalities these principles specify derive all their content and weight from their contribution to forms and aspects of human flourishing which themselves generate such conflicts. If sexual freedoms of certain sorts, say, conflict in their demands with each other, or with other freedoms, if (for example) the freedom of sexual minorities to be open about their sexual orientation conflicts with the exercise by others of freedom of association, of hiring in schools or similar institutions, there is no way these conflicts can be settled without appeal to the impact the various freedoms will have on human well-being; and any assessment of this impact is bound to invoke judgements of the relative weight of human interests that involve intractably disputed conceptions of the good life and incommensurabilities within even those aspects of such conceptions that are not contested but are held in common. The conventional liberal view neglects the vital fact that, if true, value-pluralism is a death-blow to the Kantian project of a pure philosophy of right. It is equally fatal to Lockean theories of fundamental rights, and to the account of natural law which such theories necessarily rest upon. For Berlin, certainly, value-pluralism is not restricted to conceptions of the good. It goes all the way down, right down into principles of justice and rights.

If Berlin's value-pluralism applies to principles of right as well as to conceptions of the good, is not the common charge of relativism against him a strong one? This is a potentially far more serious objection, which has been well stated by Sandel. Referring to the passage from *Four Essays on Liberty* quoted at the start of this chapter, in which Berlin quotes 'an admirable writer of our time', in fact Joseph Schumpeter, as saying 'To realize the relative validity of one's convictions and yet stand for them unflinchingly, is what distinguishes a civilized man from a barbarian,' Sandel asks: 'If one's convictions are only relatively valid, why stand for them unflinchingly? In a tragically configured moral universe, such as Berlin assumes, is the ideal of freedom any less subject than competing ideals to the ultimate incommensurability of values? If so, in what can its privileged status consist? And if freedom has no morally privileged status, if it is just one value among many, then what can be said for liberalism?'[8] According to Sandel, Berlin 'comes perilously close to foundering on the relativist predicament'.

This objection of Sandel's is in fact not one argument but two. There is first the familiar claim, which Leo Strauss had earlier advanced with characteristic obtuseness and perversity,[9] that Berlin is a relativist. This is merely the dogmatic assertion that objective pluralism in ethics, the position Berlin has always defended, is an impossibility. It has been well answered by Michael Walzer, when he says that pluralism 'can indeed be borne, can even be celebrated as the necessary outcome of human freedom and creativity. But this celebration does not entail relativism – for two reasons: first, because the discovery of a pluralist universe is a real discovery; there really are many visions and many ways, self-validating and uncombinable; and second, because the freedom that gives rise to these visions and ways is genuinely valuable.'[10] This familiar criticism of Strauss's need detain us no further.[11] It is entirely distinct from the truly serious objection that nothing in Berlin's thought privileges liberalism. For, of course, there are many non-relativist thinkers who are not liberals – the vast majority of classical moral and political philosophers, starting with Aristotle, fall clearly into this category. It is true that, if Berlin were a relativist, liberalism could have no special authority; but this is a trivial and uninteresting observation. In order to resist the second, and substantive objection of Sandel's, that nothing in Berlin's pluralism shows why freedom of choice should not be only one value among others, we need to do far more than show that he is not a relativist; we need to show how value-pluralism of the sort Berlin defends is compatible with, or even supports, the primacy of freedom of choice, which, on Berlin's account, as on others, is constitutive of liberalism. Can this be done?

Berlin's own statements on the relations of pluralism with liberalism are not entirely of one voice. He has asserted that the two doctrines are 'not the same or even overlapping concepts', indeed 'they are not logically connected'.[12] At the same time, he has said that 'Pluralism entails . . . a minimum degree of toleration . . .'[13] And in a recent paper co-authored with Bernard Williams, Berlin has sought to resist arguments claiming to show that the truth of pluralism undermines any rational argument for liberalism and renders the liberal form of life merely one option among others.[14] It will be my strategy of interpretation to assume that both the claim that pluralism entails liberalism and the claim that they are wholly distinct and independent doctrines can be given textual support from Berlin's writings. Similarly, and in virtue of this first assumption, I will take it that both the thesis that liberalism has a universal claim on reason in virtue of the nature of man as a choice-making creature, and the thesis that liberalism is a moral and political commitment with no universal claim on reason, can be found in his writings. The question of interpretation of Berlin, given that the textual evidences are not wholly unequivocal, is second in importance to the question of substance: Does value-pluralism support liberalism, or can the two come into conflict with one another?

I have already noted three strands of reasoning whereby value-pluralism might support liberal values and practices, especially those associated with negative liberty and toleration. It remains to consider how pluralism and liberalism might be competitive. There seem to be three arguments in support of the counter-claim that such competition is not merely possible, but actually inescapable. Let us consider first the last of the three arguments which aim to link value-pluralism with liberalism – the argument that authoritarian or illiberal societies or regimes are bound to deny the truth of value-pluralism. This is true only of those illiberal orders which ground themselves on the Western universalist premises that the truth of value-pluralism demolishes. It is true that value-pluralism undermines the universalist claims made by illiberal societies that are Marxist, utilitarian or positivist, Platonist, Christian or Muslim, at their foundations; but human history to date, and the human prospect for the likely future, abounds with illiberal cultures that are particularistic, not universalistic, in the values they claim to embody. Authoritarian regimes sustained by Hindu, Shinto or Orthodox Jewish doctrine, or which seek simply to preserve a local way of life, make none of the universal claims that value-pluralism subverts. All that needs to be claimed on behalf of such illiberal societies is that they harbour worthwhile forms of life which will be compromised, or destroyed, by the exercise of freedom of choice. If this once be admitted, why should the value of unimpeded choice always trump that of the forms of life that are undone by such choice? How *could* it, if value-pluralism is true?

The counter-claim to the third argument from pluralism

to liberalism is that particularistic illiberal regimes are not committed to asserting the unique or universal authority of the ways of life which they protect, nor are they committed to denying the value of other ways of life, such as other non-liberal particularisms, or (for that matter) liberal forms of life. Indeed, because particularistic cultures eschew universalistic reasonings, they would – contrary to the line of argument we are considering – appear particularly well placed to perceive and accept the truth of value-pluralism, and its corollary, the worth and validity of radically different forms of life. It is universalist regimes that have difficulty in this regard.

The second line of argument from pluralism to liberalism fares no better. Indeed it cuts the other way. If liberal societies are to be commended on the pluralist ground that they harbour more genuine values than some illiberal societies, does it not follow that the human world will be still richer in value if it contains not only liberal societies but also illiberal regimes that shelter worthwhile forms of life that would otherwise perish? To hold that only liberal ways of life are valuable, or that they are always more valuable than illiberal ways of life, is to ascribe to freedom of choice a pre-eminent value that is undefended and implausible – especially if the truth of value-pluralism is assumed. It is to say that, when the preservation or extension of diversity in valuable forms of life conflicts with negative freedom, it is always the former that must yield. But if diversity comes into conflict with liberty, and the diversity is that of worthwhile forms of life expressive of genuine human needs and embodying authentic varieties of human flourishing, why should liberty always trump diversity – especially if one is a value-pluralist? To claim that it must do so is to say that no form of life deserves to survive if it cannot withstand the force of the exercise of free choice by its members. But this is precisely the pure philosophy of right that Berlinian value-pluralism undercuts.

The argument from pluralism to liberalism might at this

point fall back on the first of the three chains of reasoning – that which holds that, if values are truly incommensurable, then there can never be good reason to justify imposing any particular ranking of them on anyone. This is perhaps the simplest, and probably potentially the most powerful of the three arguments, since it aims directly to derive the privileged status of choice from value-pluralism. Unfortunately it too fails. For a particularistic illiberal regime need not claim, when it imposes a particular ranking of incommensurable values on its subjects, that this ranking is uniquely rational, or even that it is a better ranking than others that are presently found in the world. It need only claim that it is a ranking embedded in, and necessary for the survival of, a particular way of life that is itself worthwhile, and that this ranking, and the way of life it supports, would be imperilled by the unimpeded exercise of choice. In other words, a particularistic regime which imposes a particular ranking of incommensurable values on its subjects will claim no unique or special justification for that ranking. It claims rational justification, not for the peculiar ranking of incommensurable values it imposes, but for its action in protecting that ranking as an essential element in a worthwhile way of life. This is, after all, a claim often, and not unreasonably, made in liberal societies, when they seek to justify the legal non-recognition of polygamous marriage, say, not by any claim about the peculiar value of monogamous marriage, but by the role monogamous marriage has in a particular way of life that is worth renewing. If such an argument has force in its applications in liberal societies, why should it not also have force in regard to whole ways of life that are non-liberal? How could a value-pluralist conceivably resist the larger force of this argument?

It is no answer to say that illiberal ways of life can exist as enclaves within liberal societies, since, though this is true to a degree, such enclaves are not the entire ways of life that produced them, and they may well lack many of the virtues of their parent cultures. This common liberal response neglects the plain fact that liberal societies tend to drive out non-liberal forms of life, to ghettoize or marginalize them, or to trivialize them. It passes over the commonplace truth that, even if pre-liberal virtues linger on in liberal societies, they do so as shadows of their former selves, incompletely realized in those who exhibit them. This commonplace is, after all, only an application of the pluralist insight that the virtues are not all combinable – not, at least, without loss to some of them; and that many genuine goods and virtues depend upon specific social structures, some of them illiberal and uncombinable with liberal societies, as their matrices. This response in no way addresses the question why, if an entire non-liberal way of life is worthwhile, it should not renew itself on its own terms, rather than those imposed on it by liberal regimes; why, if it depends on illiberal social structures as its matrix, it should not renew itself through those structures. Further, it overlooks the possibility that an illiberal regime may coherently justify to its subjects the restraints on negative freedom it imposes on them, not by reasoning – illicitly, from a value-pluralist standpoint – from the unique rationality of the pattern of incommensurable goods it thereby secures, but instead from the worth of the particular way of life that is thereby protected. The argument from pluralism to liberalism fails, in each of the variants we have considered, because the range of worthwhile forms of life is – on any assessment that is at all plausible, and certainly on any that might be made by a consistent value-pluralist – wider than any that can be contained within a liberal society.

This is not to say that it follows from the truth of pluralism that no case can be made for a liberal society – that liberalism is, so to speak, merely one item on a menu of options. To think that pluralism undermines liberalism in any such simple way is to simplify pluralism itself. Value-pluralism does not imply that there are not in particular circumstances good reasons for favouring one value, or constellation of values, over others; nor does it deny that there may be, and are, good reasons in specific historical milieux for favouring one regime over another. In our historical circumstances, for example, it may be true that the universal minimum requirements of morality have the best chance of being met under liberal institutions; and, *if* that is so, it is a very good argument for liberalism. To think otherwise, to think that the truth of pluralism disallows any argument for liberalism, is to conflate two distinct claims – the (true) pluralist doctrine that there is no common measure, or overarching principle, whereby conflicting values can be arbitrated, with the (false) sceptical doctrine which claims that where values conflict in a particular circumstance or context no reasons at all can be given for resolving the conflict in one way rather than any other. The pluralist view is rather that, in many though not in all cases, the context of cultural tradition in which conflicts of values occur will itself suggest reasons for resolving such conflicts in some ways rather than others. A blankly subjectivist result in no way follows from the truth of pluralism, which allows – and, in Berlin's case, insists – that wherever possible we should make reasonable trade-offs among conflicting goods, even where their incommensurability means that there is no principle or measure showing the unique or universal rationality of the trade-offs we make.

What does follow from the truth of pluralism is that liberal institutions can have no universal authority. Where liberal values come into conflict with others which depend for their existence on non-liberal social or political structures and forms of life, and where these values are truly incommensurables, there can – if pluralism is true – be no argument according universal priority to liberal values. To deny this is to deny the thesis of the incommensurability of values. This is what is done by those who affirm a weak version of pluralism that recognizes the uncombinability, even the constitutive uncombinability, of many human goods, while insisting on their rational comparability. Such positions seek to dissociate pluralism from incommensurability of values.[15] I do not consider this position here, partly because it is plainly not Berlin's and partly because, in order to be worth discussing, it would need some general account, akin perhaps to that of classical utilitarianism, of how rational choices are to be made among uncombinable goods. In the evident absence of any such general account we are left with the conclusion that whereas value-pluralism admits of reasonings about conflicting values in particular cases it disallows any universal principles in arbitrating their conflicts. In its application to the values embodied in liberal institutions, this implies that such liberal values can have no claim on reason that cannot be contested, or overturned, by the claims of goods that are embedded in nonliberal ways of life. It is in recognizing this truth that the agonistic liberalism I have discerned in Berlin's work distinguishes itself from all traditional species of liberal thought.

The intellectual project which Berlin's agonistic liberalism embodies is that of fusing rationalism with Romanticism, and thereby reconciling the Enlightenment with its critics in the Romantic Counter-Enlightenment. In this project the English thinker he most resembles is, of course, John Stuart Mill, in whose philosophy the inheritances of English empiricism and classical utilitarianism are at war with the influences of Romanticism and, to a degree, of German Idealism. There can be no reasonable doubt that, in its systematic pluralism, Berlin's liberalism is a far more successful synthesis than that which Mill produced. Yet the contested relations between pluralism and liberalism which are the crux of Berlin's work suggest that the synthesis attempted by Berlin is not wholly successful and that his thought remains haunted by an uncertainty. This uncertainty is intimated by the fact that his thought shows at some times the face of a deeper and subtler liberalism whose lineage is nonetheless in the tradition of John Stuart Mill and at other times a Vichian and Herderian face in which it is a critique of liberalism and of the Enlightenment, not indeed from the reactionary or traditionalist standpoint of a

Maistre or an Oakeshott, but from a standpoint of pluralism
and historicism of the sort earlier expressed in the work of
Herder and Vico. It is the historicist element in Berlin's
thought which gives the clue, I believe, to the reconciliation
of rationalism with Romantic voluntarism it seeks to
achieve, and to the status of liberalism within it.

In the course of interpreting Berlin's thought I have recurrently made reference to the element of voluntarism which
is revealed in his many affirmations that moral and political
life contain episodes of radical choice or groundless commitment. In the last chapter we saw that the central role of
will in human affairs was one of the ideas of the Romantic
Counter-Enlightenment that was taken up in our time by
movements which sought to deny altogether the rational
and moral unity of mankind. In our century, the most
powerful forms of such particularism have been radical and
modernist, not traditionalist – the fascist doctrines and
movements, based on race or nation, which traded on ideas
of authenticity and of the primacy of will derived from
Romanticism. In so far as these radical movements sought
to release the particular forms of life which they sponsored
from all common human standards, as at least some among
them – notably National Socialism – plainly did, it is clear
that they sought the destruction, or at any rate the suppression, of that universal framework of categories and
norms of moral thought that Berlin has always adumbrated.
However much the content of the substantive moral norms
they are embodied in may vary over time and from culture
to culture, these norms – of fairness and consideration for
others' interests, for example – form the common horizon
of the species, in Berlin's conception of it, such that beyond
it there is only unintelligibility, or at any rate nothing consistent with even the minimum content of morality. The
really radical particularist movements of our time were
committed to blotting out this common human horizon.
They are for that reason condemned by what may be termed
the minimal universalism of Berlin's thought.

The common moral horizon of the species may disqualify the most radical forms of particularism; it does not, however, ground or privilege liberalism. Radical particularism is further limited in its claims by another element in Berlin's thought which distinguishes it from the most full-blooded Romantic doctrines – which is its recognition that self-creation occurs always in the context of a specific cultural inheritance. The choosing self in Berlin is never, even when the choices it makes are radical choices, an unencumbered or abstract self; it is a self whose identity is constituted by particular allegiances, cultural traditions and communal memberships, however complex and plural. Even the self engaged in self-creation through radical choice-making does not invent itself *ex nihilo*. This is to reduce greatly the role of will from the apotheosis it achieves in the thought of Fichte or Nietzsche and all the more radical forms of Romanticism. Neither individual identities, nor forms of common cultural life, can be radically voluntaristic creations of acts of will, since both individuals and peoples are pervaded in their thoughts and sentiments by inheritances of language and practice which shape and mould them in profound and manifold ways. To note this is to note another point, which may be of some importance. Radical choice, or groundless decision, in the sense of self-defining actions for which reasons are not, and often cannot, be given may have all the importance in human life Berlin ascribes to them. Yet they are often, perhaps typically, not best characterized as acts of will, but rather as retrospective reconstructions of human experience, which constitute it in a new form for the future. In other words, radical choices may well not be reason-based and yet not be acts of will. Indeed, if Romantic expressivism is true, most radical choices cannot be acts of will; they must rather be expressions, perhaps novel ones, of identities and forms of life that the choosing self already partakes of. In this sense self-creation by choice-making, even by the making of radical choices, goes on all the while; but only rarely in the form of making acts of will.

The formation of the chooser by language and a particular history, by a particular cultural inheritance, limits the possibilities of radical Romantic voluntarism; but again it does not privilege liberalism, any more than does Berlin's conception of the common human horizon of values. For the particular selves which engage in self-creation by choice-making are themselves deposits of common forms of life. In so far as they renew these forms of life through their choices, negative freedom will be significant to them primarily in so far as it is an element of the form of life they renew through their choices. The value of negative freedom in Berlin's thought is as a condition of self-creation through choice-making. The selves that are created, or amended, through choice-making, may or may not be selves which need negative freedom for their continued self-creation. Choice-making, after all, goes on, even in the absence of negative freedom; it is, as Berlin reminds us, an inescapable necessity of the human condition. Once again, the link between pluralism and liberalism – in this case through negative liberty – is broken. What has been effectively dispelled is the radically voluntarist conception of the unencumbered self, creating itself as it goes along by acts of will unmediated by any constitutive cultural inheritance.

The recognition that most radical choices cannot be acts of will is entirely consistent with the tenor of Berlin's thought on this matter. It remains true that acts of will do have a place in Berlin's agonistic liberalism that is denied them in most species of liberal rationalism. This is recognized by Berlin himself, when – as if qualifying the statement 'Fundamentally, I am a liberal rationalist', made in an earlier interview[16] – he asserts 'In a sense I am an existentialist – that's to say I commit myself, or find that I am in fact committed, to constellations of certain values.'[17] This is because the weights of the constellations of incommensurable values of which he speaks are not given by nature or by culture, but must be conferred upon them by choice. The constellation of values itself, however, is a matter of cultural inheritance; it is that contingent history which makes the choosing self the particular chooser it is. What limits radical voluntarism in Berlin's thought, accordingly, is much more the historicity of the choosing subject than the common horizon of human values. And, though this is a development of his thought that Berlin himself might well reject, it is in the historical reality of a human subject which conceives choice-making to be centrally constitutive of its identity, rather than in any supposed universal inference from the truth of value-pluralism to the supreme value of choice itself, that liberalism is best grounded, if a ground for it be sought.

This is to say that there is no direct or universal road from the idea of man as a species whose nature is transformed through the recurrent exercise of powers of choice-making to the ideal of a society in which the making of choices is conceived to be central to the human good.[18] Indeed the two notions have no necessary connections of any sort with one another. The key element in the conception of man as a species whose nature is only partly determinate, as it is advanced by Berlin, is the assertion of the historical variability of human nature, and the related claim that it is through cultural difference that human beings acquire particular identities. For the most part, cultural identities are formed through choice-making, only if we understand 'choice' in a very extended sense, as referring to the countless adjustments in behaviour people make, often without deliberation or even reflection, to their various inheritances and changing circumstances. ('Choice' is here as open-textured a term as 'value'.) In some circumstances, however, agents may find themselves compelled to choose between whole cultural traditions, or forms of life – as when the choice of a marriage partner carries with it acceptance of a particular religion, a specific place in a social structure. In such cases, cultural difference is indeed an expression of radical choice. Even where choice is radical and central in such ways in the formation of cultural identities, nothing follows as to the value of the activity of choice. Often enough, the forms of life so chosen are ones in which choice-making is accorded no special significance. The elevation of choice-making to a central place in the human good cannot, then, be a deduction from a universal feature of human life, namely the role that choosing has in making us the people we are; nor can it be derived from the pluralist thesis of value-incommensurability.

If the supreme value of choice-making cannot, for the reasons developed earlier, be derived from the pluralist thesis of value-incommensurability, if that thesis is indeed incompatible with any claim that freedom of choice has universal and pre-eminent value, then the ground of liberalism must instead be found in a particular cultural tradition or form of life in which choice-making is central to the good life. This cultural tradition is that of the liberal societies themselves, in which self-creation through choice-making is a valued activity, and restraint of the negative freedom to engage in this activity is resented and stands in need of justification. On this view, which is not Berlin's, but which I am arguing best coheres with the historicist turn of his thought, there can be, and need be, no universal justification for liberalism. It neither possesses nor requires 'foundations'. It is instead best understood as a particular form of life, practised by people who have a certain self-conception, in which the activity of unfettered choice is central.

An interpretation of Berlinian liberalism in these historicist terms has been given by Richard Rorty. Commenting on Berlin's quotation from Joseph Schumpeter, cited earlier in this chapter and discussed by Sandel, Rorty comments:

> To say that convictions are only 'relatively valid' might seem to mean that they can only be justified to people who hold certain other beliefs – not to anyone and everyone. But if this were what was meant, the term would have no contrastive force, for there would be no

interesting arguments that were *absolutely* valid. Absolute validity would be confined to everyday platitudes, elementary mathematical truths, and the like; the sort of beliefs nobody wants to argue about because they are neither central to anyone's sense of who she is or what she lives for. All beliefs which are central to a person's self-image are so because their presence or absence serves as a criterion for dividing good people from bad people, the sort of person one wants to be from the sort one does not want to be. A conviction which can be justified to *anyone* is of little interest. 'Unflinching courage' will not be required to sustain such a conviction.[19]

He goes on:

> ... the assumptions usually invoked against Berlin and Schumpeter are wrong. We ... [cannot] assume that there is a largest-possible framework within which one can ask, for example, 'If freedom has no morally privileged status, if it is just one value among many, then what can be said for liberalism?' We cannot assume that liberals ought to be able to rise above the contingencies of history and see the kind of individual freedom which the modern liberal state offers its citizens as just one more value ... Only the assumption that there is some such standpoint to which we might rise gives sense to the question, 'If one's convictions are only relatively valid, why stand for them unflinchingly?'[20]

We may put Rorty's argument in the terms of our preceding discussion by noting that, aside from the common horizon of human values, values are for Berlin historic creations, embedded in particular forms of life. This is true for liberal values as for other values: their authority is local, not universal, in that it derives from a specific form of life. The historicist aspect, or implication, of Berlin's value-pluralism suggests that we forswear the enterprise of seeking universal foundations for liberalism and accept instead that it is one form of life among many that may flourish within the common human horizon of the minimal values that are universal. These latter may be specifiable by a form of philosophical inquiry which is sensitive to anthropological and historical evidences: such a naturalized and quasi-empirical Kantianism in philosophical method is often evidenced in Berlin's thought. But there is an unresolved tension in this conception of philosophy, as it is deployed in Berlin's work, generated by the strongly historicist conception of human nature with which it is precariously allied. The result of this tension is that it is never altogether clear whether the universal 'concepts and categories' that frame the common human horizon are truly cross-cultural and invariant, or whether they identify family resemblances among many, but not all, cultures. Perhaps this tension is ineliminable in Berlin's thought. Or, if it can be eliminated or transcended, it may be at a price that Berlin is reluctant to pay – that of taking further the historicist turn of his thought and applying it to philosophy itself. To do this would be to conceive philosophy after the fashion, not of Kant, but of Hegel and Collingwood, and to see it as illuminating the presuppositions of particular, historic forms of life. If this method in philosophy were adopted by him, Berlin's references to the common human horizon would be understood, not as claims about generically human modes of thought and practice, but instead as claims about resemblances within a very large and extended family of cultural forms. Philosophical inquiry would then not be a priori anthropology – as it was for Kant, say – but reflection on empirical cultural and historical anthropology. There is a good deal in Berlin's writings which lends support to this conception of philosophy.

On this conception of philosophical method, the common human horizon is bound radically to underdetermine any particular form of life, including that of liberal cultures, precisely because it is a distillation from a vast miscellany of cultures, a description of their family resemblances, not any claim about an essence they all exhibit. Philosophy will not on this view attempt to clarify the conceptual structures of all possible forms of human life; it will confine itself to those with which we are familiar, or which are readily imaginable given what we already know. If this conception of the nature and limits of philosophical inquiry be accepted as cohering with much of Berlin's thought, then philosophy cannot give a foundation to liberal practice. It can note the central role of choice-making in human life and the uncertainty and plurality of nature that choice-making confers on human beings. In so doing it will not enunciate a universal truth of anthropology, a priori or otherwise, since there may be, and indeed are, human beings who do not recognize the experience of choice as central in their lives; it will instead mark a form of life found in a great many cultures, including our own. It will further recognize the celebration of choice-making, its valorization as the benchmark of human flourishing, as a feature of some, but only some, of these cultures. (It was not so conceived by the Greeks whose moral life Aristotle theorized, for example; and it is not so understood in contemporary Confucian cultures.) It will note that most human beings, now and in the past, use their powers of self-creation to renew their identities as practitioners of non-liberal forms of life. For all these reasons, philosophical reflection will recognize ultimate and irreducible diversity in forms of life, the varieties of which are in principle unknowable, as the fundamental fact of our situation. Recognizing that these forms of life embody values – virtues, excellences, goods and so forth – that are often rationally incommensurable, philosophy will not seek to privilege any one form of life. This is the logic of Berlin's argument, if value-pluralism indeed goes all the way down, and applies to the value of choice-making itself.

On this view, the agonistic character of Berlin's liberalism is exemplified not only in the conflicts of rivalrous goods it admits and celebrates, but in the fact that it is itself a form of partisanship, which depends for its survival in a world that has never been friendly to it on the commitment and wilful energy of its practitioners, and on nothing else. This is the ineradicable voluntarist element in Berlin's thought – that the relation we have to liberal practices is in the nature of a groundless commitment. It is true that we recognize ourselves, we find our self-conception mirrored, in those practices; but we confirm that identity and its participation in those practices, when both are challenged by other identities and other practices that are not liberal, by an act of commitment. It is true that, within a liberal form of life, we can give indefinitely many reasons for our choices; but, when our form of life is confronted by another which is radically different but which harbours many human goods and excellences, our spade is turned. (I leave aside here the possibility that some non-liberal ways of life may protect the universal minimum content of morality better than some liberal forms of life, except to note that this possibility shows that liberal forms of life are not on the account being sketched here supposed to be beyond criticism.) The liberal *agon* of rivalrous goods occurs in a form of life surrounded by others that are *its* rivals. Agonistic liberalism, on this interpretation of Berlin's thought, presupposes the yet deeper conflicts among forms of life that are encompassed in agonistic pluralism. It is such an agonistic pluralism that is advocated by Herder – though with a charming *naïveté* as to the peaceful means whereby conflicts among forms of life will be prosecuted – and which is suggested by Machiavelli.[21]

That it is agonistic pluralism that is the bottom line in Berlin's thought is suggested by his criticisms of the Whiggish interpretation of history that informed the Enlightenment. Against the Enlightenment expectation that human beings would converge on a universal identity as members of a cosmopolitan civilization Berlin asserts the truth of a pluralistic expressivism – that the disposition of human beings to constitute for themselves identities and ways of life that are partly defined by their exclusion of others is very strong and likely to be as prominent in the human future as in the past. To suppose that human beings will converge on a liberal form of life, or to think that such a form of life is most expressive of their essential nature, is to suppress all the insights into the essential indeterminacy of human nature, and into the propensity of human beings to invent diverse identities for themselves, that Berlin finds in Herder. If, as I think is the truth, agonistic liberalism is in Berlin's thought a special case of agonistic pluralism, so that the former presupposes the latter, then when the two come into ultimate conflict it is liberalism that is bound to yield.

The best exemplar of a thinker for whom agonistic liberalism is only a special case of agonistic pluralism is not John Stuart Mill but Alexander Herzen. Of Herzen's outlook Berlin writes:

> This denunciation of general moral rules – without a trace of Byronic or Nietzschean hyperbole – is a doctrine not heard often in the nineteenth century; indeed, in its full extent, not until well into our own. It hits both left and right; against the romantic historians, against Hegel, and to some extent against Kant; against utilitarians, and against supermen; against Tolstoy, and against the religion of art, against 'scientific ethics', and all the churches; it is empirical and naturalistic, recognizes absolute values as well as change, and is overawed neither by evolution nor by socialism. And it is original to an arresting degree.[22]

With due allowance made for the passage of time, these same words could as easily apply to Berlin himself. The outlook they express, which I have called – infelicitously enough, no doubt – agonistic pluralism is hardly likely to be less appropriate to our needs at a time when the historical theodicies of the political religions, such as Marxism, have been supplanted by resurgent fundamentalisms as threats both to individual liberty and minimal human decency. At any rate, this agonistic pluralism is, it seems to me, the deepest truth in Berlin's thought, and its consequence – that liberal society is only one form of human flourishing, one to which Berlin himself is steadfastly committed, but which has no apodictic status within his thought – is one we are bound to accept. It is in this connection noteworthy that when, in a comprehensive retrospective assessment of his thought, Berlin asks what are the implications for practice of the pluralism of values he has long insisted upon, it is not liberalism, but moderation and compromise that he dwells upon:

> If the old perennial belief in the possibility of realizing ultimate harmony is a fallacy, and the positions of the thinkers I have appealed to – Machiavelli, Vico, Herder, Herzen – are valid, if we allow that the Great Goods can collide, that some of them cannot live together, even though others can – in short, that one cannot have everything, in principle as well as in practice – and if human creativity may depend upon a variety of mutually exclusive choices: then, as Chernyshevsky and Lenin once asked, 'What is to be done? How are we to choose between possibilities? What and how much are we to sacrifice to what?' There is, it seems to me, no clear reply . . . The best that can be done, as a general rule, is to maintain a precarious equilibrium that will prevent the occurrence of desperate situations, of intolerable choices – that is the first requirement for a decent society.[23]

In this pluralistic view it is the recognition of the ultimate validity of conflicting claims, rather than the special claims of liberty, that is most stressed: 'Claims can be balanced, compromises can be reached: in concrete situations not every claim is of equal force – so much liberty and so much equality; so much for sharp moral condemnation, and so much for understanding a given human situation; so much for the full force of the law, and so much for the prerogative of mercy; for feeding the hungry, clothing the naked, healing the sick, sheltering the homeless. Priorities, never final and absolute, must be established.'[24] This emphasis on the mediation of value-conflict, on avoiding, where possible, occasions for radical and tragic choice, on balance and compromise, has been criticized as a retreat from the most radical implications of value-pluralism;[25] but it seems to me an entirely reasonable application by Berlin of his pluralist master-idea. Its implication – not, to be sure, one Berlin himself draws – is that liberal society is one, but only one form, of life that human beings may adopt, once they have achieved the minimal conditions of decency among themselves. Accordingly, the commitment to the liberal form of life – like that to any form of life that meets the minimal standards of decency – is a groundless one, which nothing in reason compels us to make. If value-pluralism is true all the way down, then it follows inexorably that the identity of practitioners of a liberal form of life is a contingent matter, not a privileged expression of universal human nature. If there is value-conflict all the way down, then there is contingency all the way down, too.

Berlin's central idea of pluralism in ultimate values denies human beings the metaphysical comfort, itself answering to a nearly universal human need, whereby their particular forms of life are accorded a universal authority by being underwritten or guaranteed by a rational or natural or historical order. Berlin's thought does not satisfy, or seek to appease, this human need for metaphysical consolation. If anything it does the opposite. It returns us to mortal men and women, in all their unconsoled sorrow, cleaving to them in their natural defiance of the mocking harmonies of all theodicies. In this Berlin's voice is akin to that of Job, in refusing with a passion the pretence that there is peace when our lives abound in deep conflicts and hard choices. It is in its character as an anti-theodicy, and in its drawing out the implications for moral and political life of the incoherence of the very idea of perfection, that the unique and permanent achievement of Berlin's thought is to be found.

Notes

INTRODUCTION

1 Claude Galipeau's excellent *Isaiah Berlin's Liberalism* (Oxford, Oxford University Press, 1994) has remedied this strange defect. I have learnt much from Galipeau's fine study and am much indebted to it.
2 See 'The Three Strands in My Life' in *The Jewish Quarterly*, vol. 27 (1979).
3 R. Jahanbegloo, *Conversations with Isaiah Berlin* (London, Peter Halban, 1992), p. 49.
4 Noel Annan, *Our Age* (London, Fontana, 1991), p. 378.

CHAPTER 1

1 I. Berlin, *Against the Current* (London, Hogarth Press, 1979), p. 157.
2 See M. Oakeshott, *Rationalism in Politics and Other Essays* (Indianapolis, Liberty Press, 1991).
3 I. Berlin, 'The Purpose of Philosophy' in his *Concepts and Categories* (London, Hogarth Press, 1978), p. 11.
4 See, especially, Joseph Raz, *The Morality of Freedom* (Oxford, Clarendon Press, 1986).
5 I. Berlin, *Four Essays on Liberty* (London, Oxford University Press, 1969), p. xiii.
6 J. S. Mill, *A System of Logic*, vi. ii, 'Of Liberty and Necessity'.
7 G. Strawson, *Freedom and Belief* (Oxford, Oxford University Press, 1991).
8 *Four Essays*, pp. xxiii–xxiv.
9 Berlin's most extended and systematic argument to this conclusion is in his paper, 'The Concept of Scientific History', in *Concepts and Categories*, pp. 103–42.
10 See, for this, K. R. Popper, *The Poverty of Historicism* (London, Routledge & Kegan Paul, 1957); and *The Open Society and Its Enemies*, 5th ed., (London, Routledge & Kegan Paul, 1966).
11 *Concepts and Categories*, p. 80.
12 *Concepts and Categories*, pp. 162–3.
13 See Stuart Hampshire, *Thought and Action* (London, Chatto & Windus, 1970); P. F. Strawson, *Freedom and Resentment* (London, Methuen, 1974).
14 I. Berlin, *Four Essays*, p. 169.
15 See Charles Taylor, 'What's Wrong with Negative Liberty' in Alan Ryan, ed., *The Idea of Freedom: Essays in Honour of Isaiah Berlin* (Oxford, Oxford University Press, 1979).
16 *Concepts and Categories*, p. 149.
17 John Rawls, *A Theory of*

Justice (Oxford, Oxford University Press, 1972).

18 See Jahanbegloo, *Conversations with Isaiah Berlin*, p. 41.

19 *Four Essays*, pp. 131–2.

20 G. C. McCallum, *Philosophical Review*, vol. 76, no. 3 (1967), pp. 312–34.

21 Joel Feinberg, *Social Philosophy* (Eaglewood Cliffs, NJ, Prentice-Hall, 1973).

22 *Four Essays*, pp. xliii.

23 *Four Essays*, p. lvi.

24 *Four Essays*, p. 127.

25 *Four Essays*, pp. 153–4.

26 *Four Essays*, p. 130, footnote 1.

27 See *Four Essays*, p. 123: 'It is only because I believe that my inability to get a given thing is due to the fact that other human beings have made arrangements whereby I am, whereas others are not, prevented from having enough money with which to pay for it, that I think myself a victim of coercion or slavery. In other words, this use of the term depends on a particular social and economic theory about the causes of my poverty or weakness.' I discuss the issues raised by this statement of Berlin's in my *Liberalisms: Essays in Political Philosophy* (London: Routledge, 1989), chapter 4, pp. 61–2.

28 *Four Essays*, p. 123.

29 See Felix Oppenheim, *Dimensions of Freedom* (New York, St Martin's Press, 1961).

30 *Four Essays*, p. 169: 'The necessity of choosing between absolute claims is then an inescapable characteristic of the human condition. This gives its

value to freedom as Acton had conceived of it – as an end in itself . . .'

31 Raz, *The Morality of Freedom*.

32 Ibid., p. 345.

33 See my *Beyond the New Right: Markets, Government and the Common Environment* (London and New York, Routledge, 1993), chapter 3.

34 For the role of the idea of a quiddity, or individual nature, in Mill's liberalism, see my *Mill on Liberty: A Defence* (London, Routledge & Kegan Paul, 1983).

35 See Loren E. Lomasky, *Persons, Rights and the Moral Community* (Oxford, Clarendon Press, 1987), for its critique of the ideal of autonomy.

36 'From Hope and Fear Set Free', *Concepts and Categories*, pp. 173–98.

37 John Rawls, *Political Liberalism* (New York, Columbia University Press, 1993).

38 Raz, *The Morality of Freedom*, chapter 5.

39 Ibid., chapter 8.

40 For the idea of a species of Aristotelian ethics that is radically pluralistic, see Stuart Hampshire's *Freedom of Mind* (Oxford, Clarendon Press, 1972), pp. 63–86, 'A Defence of Aristotle'.

41 D. Gauthier, *Morals by Agreement* (Oxford, Clarendon Press, 1986), pp. 353–5.

42 I have considered some of the implications of ideals of autonomy for liberalism in my *Beyond the New Right*, chapter 3; and in my *Post-liberalism: Studies in Political Thought*

(New York and London, Routledge, 1993), chapter 20.

43 I discuss some of these issues arising from the disputed relations of pluralism with liberalism in 'What is Dead and What is Living in Liberalism' in my *Post-liberalism*, chapter 20.

CHAPTER 2

1 I. Berlin, *Vico and Herder: Two Studies in the History of Ideas* (London, Hogarth Press, 1976), pp. 206–7.

2 A. MacIntyre, *Whose Justice? Which Rationality?* (London, Duckworth, 1988), p. 142.

3 Berlin acknowledges in several places that the foundational commitment to the necessary compatibility, or even the mutual entailment of values, predates Socrates.

4 'The Originality of Machiavelli' in *Against the Current*, pp. 67–8.

5 Ibid., pp. 78–9.

6 Ibid., p. 79.

7 Jahanbegloo, *Conversations with Isaiah Berlin*, p. 44: 'Pluralism and liberalism are not the same or even overlapping concepts. There are liberal theories which are not pluralistic. I believe in both liberalism and pluralism, but they are not logically connected.'

8 Evidence for its elusiveness, and of how easily it is misunderstood, is found in Gerald C. McCallum's paper on 'Berlin on the Compatibility of Ideals and "Ends"', *Ethics* (1967), pp. 139–45. MacCallum's misunderstandings of Berlin

have been well criticized by G. A. Cohen in his paper, 'A Note on Values and Sacrifices', *Ethics*, vol. 79 (1969), pp. 159–62.

There is a substantial, and growing, philosophical literature on the subject of value-incommensurability. The most illuminating contributions of which I am aware are: Joseph Raz, *The Morality of Freedom* (Oxford, Oxford University Press, 1988), pp. 321–66; Michael Stocker, *Plural and Conflicting Values* (Oxford, Oxford University Press, 1992); James Griffin, *Well-Being* (Oxford, Oxford University Press, 1988), chapter 5, and 'Mixing Values' in *Proceedings of the Aristotelian Society*, supplementary vol. 65 (1991); Charles Taylor, 'The Diversity of Goods' in C. Taylor, ed., *Philosophy and the Human Sciences* (Cambridge University Press, 1985); A. K. Sen, 'Plural Utility' in *Proceedings of the Aristotelian Society*, 1981; Bernard Williams, 'Conflict of Values' in his *Moral Luck* (Cambridge, Cambridge University Press, 1981); John Finnis, *Fundamentals of Ethics* (Oxford, Oxford University Press, 1992), pp. 89 et. seq.; Thomas Nagel, 'The Fragmentation of Value' in his *Mortal Questions* (Cambridge, Canto, new edn, 1991); Martha Nussbaum, 'Plato on Commensurability and Desire' in *Love's Knowledge* (New York, Oxford University Press, 1992), pp. 106–32; John Kekes, *The Morality of Pluralism* (Princeton, Princeton University Press, 1993); Steven Lukes, 'On Trade-offs Between Values',

European University Institute Working Papers in Political and Social Sciences, Paper no. 92/94 (European University Institute, Florence, August 1992).

9 Raz, *The Morality of Freedom*, pp. 335–45.

10 Ibid., p. 234.

11 Ibid., p. 322.

12 Ibid., p. 325.

13 Ibid., p. 326.

14 Ibid., p. 327.

15 Ibid., p. 334.

16 J. Raz, 'Multiculturalism: A Liberal Perspective', in *Ethics in the Public Domain* (Oxford, Clarendon Press, 1994), chapter 7, pp. 155–76.

17 Stuart Hampshire, *Innocence and Experience* (London, Penguin Press, 1989), p. 108.

18 See, especially, Bernard Williams, *Ethics and the Limits of Philosophy* (London, Fontana Press/HarperCollins, 1985).

19 I discuss the breakdown in transitivity in judgements of evils in my book, *Post-liberalism*, pp. 303–4.

20 *Four Essays*, p. lvi.

21 See Derek Parfit, *Reasons and Persons* (Oxford, Clarendon Press, 1984).

22 See my *Mill on Liberty*, p. 120.

23 *Four Essays*, p. 194.

24 The expression 'compossible rights' is due, I believe, to Hillel Steiner. See H. Steiner, *An Essay on Rights* (Oxford, Blackwell, 1994).

25 The idea of a side-constraint is invoked, but not explained, in Robert Nozick's *Anarchy, State and Utopia*

(Oxford, Basil Blackwell, 1974), pp. 26–30.

26 See John Rawls, *Political Liberalism*.

27 R. Dworkin, *Law's Empire* (Cambridge, Mass., Harvard University Press, 1986); and his earlier *Taking Rights Seriously* (London, Duckworth, 1977).

28 Bernard Williams, 'Introduction', in I. Berlin, *Concepts and Categories*, p. xviii.

29 J. Raz, *The Morality of Freedom*, pp. 345–53.

30 H. L. A. Hart, *The Concept of Law* (Oxford, Clarendon Press, 1961), pp. 189–95.

31 R. Wollheim, 'The Idea of a Common Human Nature', in E. and A. Margalit, eds., *Isaiah Berlin: A Celebration* (London, Hogarth Press, 1991), p. 69.

32 *Concept and Categories*, pp. 164–5.

33 Ibid., p. 166.

34 See, for this characterization of philosophy, 'The Purpose of Philosophy', in *Concepts and Categories*, pp. 1–11.

35 For a brief deployment of the idea of internal realism in relation to value-incommensurability, see my *Post-liberalism*, pp. 297–8.

36 This must be so, if only because the natural languages we learn in infancy are historical creations.

37 I develop this point somewhat in my *Post-liberalism*, pp. 322–6.

38 That both language and history are necessarily plural is a feature of the thought of Michael Oakeshott. The

contrasts between this and Berlin's are as instructive as the – often neglected, but easily exaggerated – similarities.

CHAPTER 3

1 *Concepts and Categories,* pp. 141–2.

2 *Against the Current*, p. 129.

3 *Four Essays*, pp. 71–2.

4 See K. R. Popper, *The Poverty of Historicism.*

5 See Stuart Hampshire, *Freedom of Mind.*

6 On this see P. L. Gardiner, *The Nature of Historical Explanation* (Oxford, Oxford University Press, 1952).

7 See K. R. Popper, *The Open Society and Its Enemies.*

8 Stuart Hampshire, 'Nationalism', in *Isaiah Berlin: A Celebration*, p. 129.

9 A rather different interpretation of Hume's account of history and human nature is advanced by Donald Livingstone in his *Hume's Philosophy of Common Life* (Chicago, University of Chicago Press, 1984).

10 For instance, G. A. Cohen's restatement of Marxian historical materialism in functionalist terms in his *Karl Marx's Theory of History: A Defence* (Oxford, Oxford University Press, 1978).

11 See his essay on 'Historical Inevitability' in *Four Essays on Liberty*, especially pp. 51–5.

12 I. Berlin, 'The Hedgehog and the Fox', in his *Russian Thinkers* (London, Penguin Books, 1979), pp. 41–2.

13 I. Berlin, 'Tolstoy and Enlightenment', in *Russian Thinkers*, p. 254.

14 See L. Trotsky, 'Their Morals and Ours'.

15 The idea of the evanescence of particularism was, for the most *simpliste* Enlightenment thinkers, part of their conception of the evanescence of imperfection. On this, see my *Post-liberalism*, p. 299.

16 See I. Berlin, *New York Review of Books*, November 21, 1991, pp. 19–23.

17 S. Hampshire, *Innocence and Experience*, new edition (London, Penguin Books, 1992).

18 Ibid., p. 33.

19 See Stuart Hampshire, 'Justice is Strife', Presidential Address, American Philosophical Association, 1991 Pacific Division Meeting, in *Proceedings and Addresses of the American Philosophical Association*, vol. 65, no. 3 (November 1991), pp. 24–5.

20 Isaiah Berlin, *Karl Marx*, 4th ed. (Oxford, Oxford University Press, 1978), p. 14.

21 Ibid., p. 93.

22 *Four Essays on Liberty*, p. 53.

23 Ibid.

24 *Karl Marx*, p. 113.

25 G. A. Cohen, 'Isaiah's Marx, and Mine', in *Isaiah Berlin: A Celebration*, p. 125.

26 On this point I am indebted to Charles Taylor's 'The Importance of Herder', in *Isaiah Berlin: A Celebration.*

27 See C. Taylor, ibid.

28 For this project in the early Wittgenstein, see D. F. Pears, *The False Prison* (Oxford, Oxford University Press, 1987).

29 See I. Berlin, 'The Apotheosis of the Romantic Will:

The Revolt Against the Myth of an Ideal World', in his *The Crooked Timber of Humanity: Chapters in the History of Ideas* (London, John Murray, 1990).

30 The reservations have to do with his repeated assertion of the reality of a common framework of categories of human thought. It is important to note that, unlike Kant's, this is an anthropological, and a historical, not a metaphysical claim of Berlin's.

31 *Against the Current*, pp. 78–9.

32 See Quentin Skinner, *Machiavelli* (Oxford, Oxford University Press Past Masters, 1981).

CHAPTER 4

1 *Vico and Herder*, pp. 211–12.

2 See J. Raz, 'Multiculturalism: A Liberal Perspective'.

3 He did this in his *System of Logic*. See my *Mill on Liberty* for a discussion of this feature of Mill's doctrine of liberty.

4 See Michael Sandel, *Liberalism and the Limits of Justice* (Cambridge, Cambridge University Press, 1982); Alasdair MacIntyre, *After Virtue* (London, Duckworth, 1984); and Charles Taylor, *Sources of the Self* (Cambridge, Cambridge University Press, 1990).

5 Stuart Hampshire, 'Nationalism', in *Isaiah Berlin: A Celebration*, p. 128.

6 I. Berlin, 'Nationalism: Past Neglect and Present Power', in *Against the Current*, pp. 341–3.

7 I. Berlin, 'The Bent Twig: On the Rise of Nationalism', in *The Crooked Timber of Humanity*, pp. 243–4.

8 A. Margalit and J. Raz, 'National Self-determination', in *The Journal of Philosophy*, vol. 87, no. 9 (September 1990), pp. 439–61.

9 Ibid., pp. 443–7.

10 J. Raz, 'Multiculturalism: A Liberal Perspective'.

11 Ibid., p. 107.

12 Ibid.

13 S. Hampshire, 'Nationalism', p. 131.

14 Hampshire, ibid., pp. 131–2.

15 I. Berlin, 'Jewish Slavery and Emancipation', in Norman Bentwich, ed., *Hebrew University Garland* (London, Constellation Books, 1952).

16 I. Berlin, 'Benjamin Disraeli, Karl Marx and the Search for Identity', in *Against the Current*, pp. 252–86.

17 I. Berlin, 'Chaim Weizmann' in *Personal Impressions* (London, Hogarth Press, 1980), p. 42.

18 For a form of indirect utilitarianism that seeks to avoid this view, see R. Wollheim, *The Sheep and the Ceremony*, Leslie Stephen Memorial Lecture (Cambridge, Cambridge University Press, 1979).

19 S. Hampshire, *Thought and Action* (London, Chatto, 1970).

20 For an affirmation of his liberal rationalism, see R. Jahanbegloo, *Conversations with Isaiah Berlin*, p. 20.

21 In his *The Crooked Timber of Humanity*, pp. 207–37.

CHAPTER 5

1 *Against the Current*, p. 12.
2 Ibid., p. 22.
3 *The Crooked Timber of Humanity*, pp. 236–7.
4 See Berlin, 'The Counter-Enlightenment', pp. 9–10.
5 For Berlin's view of Hobbes, see R. Jahanbegloo, *Conversations with Isaiah Berlin*, pp. 61–5.
6 See I. Berlin, 'Joseph de Maistre and the Origins of Fascism', in *The Crooked Timber of Humanity*.
7 Ibid., p. 133.
8 Ibid., p. 125.
9 Ibid., p. 124.
10 Ibid., p. 102.
11 I am indebted to C. Taylor, 'The Importance of Herder', in *Isaiah Berlin: A Celebration*, for this insight.
12 I. Berlin, 'The Counter-Enlightenment', pp. 4–5.
13 I. Berlin, *The Magus of the North: J. G. Hamann and the Origins of Modern Irrationalism* (London, Murray, 1993), p. 76.
14 Ibid., p. 81.
15 L. Wittgenstein, *Philosophical Investigations* (Oxford, Basil Blackwell, 1958), Part 1, Section 242.
16 *The Magus of the North*, pp. 49–50.
17 See I. Berlin, 'Hume and the Sources of German Anti-Rationalism', in *Against the Current*, p. 182, for an account of *Glaube* in Hamann.
18 See Berlin, 'The Counter-Enlightenment', pp. 7–8.
19 *The Magus of the North*, pp. 27–8.
20 I. Berlin, *The Age of Enlightenment: The Eighteenth-Century Philosophers* (New York and Toronto, Mentor Books, 1956), p. 19.
21 *The Crooked Timber of Humanity*, p. 237.

CHAPTER 6

1 *Four Essays*, pp. lix–lx.
2 *Four Essays*, pp. 170–72.
3 S. Lukes, 'Making Sense of Moral Conflict', in Nancy Rosenblum, ed., *Liberalism and the Moral Life* (Cambridge, Mass., Harvard University Press, 1989), p. 141.
4 Introduction to *Concepts and Categories*, p. xvii.
5 Ibid., p. xviii.
6 For a good example, see Eric Mack, 'Isaiah Berlin and the Quest for Liberal Pluralism', *Public Affairs Quarterly*, vol. 7, no. 3 (July 1993).
7 See J. Rawls, *Political Liberalism*. For a good assessment of this later work of Rawls's from a standpoint that has some affinities with that of Berlin, see Stuart Hampshire, 'Liberalism: The New Twist', *New York Review of Books*, 12 August 1993, pp. 43–7.
8 Michael Sandel, 'Introduction', *Liberalism and Its Critics* (New York, New York University Press, 1984), p. 8.
9 Leo Strauss, 'Relativism', in his *The Rebirth of Classical Political Rationalism* (Chicago, University of Chicago Press, 1989), pp. 13–19.
10 Michael Walzer, 'Introduction' to Isaiah Berlin's

The Hedgehog and the Fox (New York, 1986).

11 Berlin occasionally describes the views of Vico and Herder in his book, *Vico and Herder*, as relativistic; but this is undoubtedly a *lapsus linguae*. He repudiates such a characterization explicitly in his 'Alleged Relativism in Eighteenth Century European Thought', in *The Crooked Timber of Humanity*, pp. 70–90.

12 R. Jahanbegloo, *Conversations with Isaiah Berlin*, p. 44.

13 Ibid.

14 I refer to 'Pluralism and Liberalism: A Reply' by Isaiah Berlin and Bernard Williams, *Political Studies*, vol. 42, no. 2 (June 1994), pp. 306–309. This paper is a reply to one by George Crowder entitled 'Pluralism and Liberalism', *Political Studies*, vol. 42, no. 1 (1994), pp. 293–303.

15 This is the position defended by James Griffin in his forthcoming paper, 'What's the Problem?'

16 R. Jahanbegloo, *Conversations with Isaiah Berlin*, p. 70.

17 I. Berlin, in *Between Philosophy and the History of Ideas: a conversation with Steven Lukes*, mimeo, p. 38.

18 That the conception of man as a species that transforms itself through choice-making supports a conception of the human good in which the making of choices is central is, on Berlin's interpretation of his thought, maintained or assumed by J. S. Mill. As Berlin says of Mill: 'For him man differs from animals primarily neither as the possessor of reason, nor as an inventor of tools and methods, but as a being capable of choice, one who is most himself in choosing and not being chosen for; the rider and not the horse; the seeker of ends, and not merely of means, ends that he pursues, each in his own fashion; with the corollary that the more various these fashions, the richer the lives of men become; the larger the field of interplay between individuals, the greater the opportunities of the new and unexpected; the more numerous the possibilities for altering his own character in some fresh and unexplored direction, the more paths open before each individual, and the wider will be his freedom of action and thought.' *Four Essays*, p. 178.

19 Richard Rorty, *Contingency, Irony and Solidarity* (Cambridge, Cambridge University Press, 1989), p. 47.

20 Ibid., pp. 49–50.

21 Berlin suggests that Machiavelli's pluralism, or dualism, lends support to liberalism, even against Machiavelli's will: '[Machiavelli's writings] were, by a fortunate irony of history (which some call dialectic) the bases of the very liberalism that Machiavelli would surely have condemned as feeble and characterless, lacking in single-minded pursuit of power, in splendour, in organization, in

virtu, in power to discipline
unruly men against huge odds
into one energetic whole. Yet he
is, in spite of himself, one of the
makers of pluralism, and of its –
to him – perilous acceptance of
toleration.' *Against the Current*,
p. 79.

   22 *Russian Thinkers*, p. 95.

   23 I. Berlin, 'The Pursuit of
the Ideal', in *The Crooked
Timber of Humanity*,
pp. 17–18.

   24 Ibid., p. 17.

   25 By Perry Anderson in his
'England's Isaiah', in the *London
Review of Books*, reprinted in his
Zones of Engagement (London,
Verso/New Left Books, 1992).

Further Reading

Writings by Berlin

With the exception of his biography of Marx, his anthology of the philosophers of the Enlightenment, and his study of J. G. Hamann, Isaiah Berlin's published work has taken the form of essays, often somewhat inaccessibly published in the first instance. Fortunately most of these essays have now been collected, in seven volumes published between 1969 and 1990. The contents of these volumes are listed below, under their titles.

Karl Marx: His Life and Environment appeared in 1939. The fourth edition (Oxford, Oxford University Press, 1978) was reissued by Fontana Press in 1995.

The Age of Enlightenment: The Eighteenth-Century Philosophers (New York, New American Library, 1956) is a selection, with introduction and commentary, from these philosophers' works.

Four Essays on Liberty (London, Oxford University Press, 1969):
> Introduction [a reply to his critics]
> Political Ideas in the Twentieth Century
> Historical Inevitability
> Two Concepts of Liberty
> John Stuart Mill and the Ends of Life

Vico and Herder: Two Studies in the History of Ideas (London, Hogarth Press, 1976; paperback, Chatto and Windus):
> Introduction
> The Philosophical Ideas of Giambattista Vico
> Herder and the Enlightenment

Russian Thinkers (London, Hogarth Press, 1978; paperback, Penguin):
> Introduction by Aileen Kelly
> Russia and 1848

Georges Sorel
Nationalism: Past Neglect and Present Power

Personal Impressions (London, Hogarth Press, 1980; paperback,
Oxford University Press):
  Introduction by Noel Annan
  Winston Churchill in 1940
  Hubert Henderson at All Souls
  President Franklin Delano Roosevelt
  Chaim Weizmann
  Richard Pares
  Felix Frankfurter at Oxford
  Aldous Huxley
  L. B. Namier
  Maurice Bowra
  J. L. Austin and the Early Beginnings of Oxford Philosophy
  John Petrov Plamenatz
  Auberon Herbert
  Einstein and Israel
  Meetings with Russian Writers in 1945 and 1956

*The Crooked Timber of Humanity: Chapters in the History of
Ideas* (London, John Murray, 1990; paperback, Fontana Press):
  The Pursuit of the Ideal
  The Decline of Utopian Ideas in the West
  Giambattista Vico and Cultural History
  Alleged Relativism in Eighteenth-Century European
    Thought
  European Unity and its Vicissitudes
  Joseph de Maistre and the Origins of Fascism
  The Apotheosis of the Romantic Will:
    The Revolt against the Myth of an Ideal World
  The Bent Twig: On the Rise of Nationalism

*The Magus of the North: J. G. Hamann and the Origins of Modern
Irrationalism* (London, John Murray, 1993; paperback, Fontana
Press).

These are the books that Berlin has so far published. Readers who
wish to explore the many pieces not yet collected in volume form
should consult the complete bibliography of Berlin's writings by

Henry Hardy, who has compiled and edited all the volumes published from 1978 onwards (jointly, in the case of *Russian Thinkers*, with Aileen Kelly). This bibliography appears in its currently most up-to-date published form in the 1991 impression of the Oxford University Press paperback edition of *Against the Current.*

Writings about Berlin

The list of publications stimulated by Berlin's ideas is growing steadily. There are two collections published in his honour:

Alan Ryan, ed., *The Idea of Freedon: Essays in Honour of Isaiah Berlin* (Oxford, Oxford University Press, 1979)

Edna and Avishai Margalit, eds., *Isaiah Berlin: A Celebration* (London, Hogarth Press, 1991)

In addition to the present volume, two other book-length studies of Berlin's thought have so far appeared in English:

Robert Kocis, *A Critical Appraisal of Sir Isaiah Berlin's Political Philosophy* (Lewiston, NY, etc., Edwin Mellen Press, 1989)

Claude J. Galipeau, *Isaiah Berlin's Liberalism* (Oxford, Clarendon Press, 1994)

Among the many articles on Berlin, or on topics treated by him, the following may be of special interest to readers of this book:

Bhikhu Parekh, 'Isaiah Berlin', chapter 2 in his *Contemporary Political Thinkers* (Oxford, Martin Robertson, 1982)

Roger Hausheer, 'Berlin and the Emergence of Liberal Pluralism', in Pierre Manent and others, *European Liberty: Four Essays on the Occasion of the 25th Anniversary of the Erasmus Prize Foundation* (The Hague etc., Martinus Nijhoff, 1983)

John Gray, 'On Negative and Positive Liberty', chapter 4 in *Liberalisms: Essays in Political Philosophy* (London and New York, Routledge, 1989)

John Gray, 'Berlin's Agonistic Liberalism', chapter 6 in *Post-liberalism: Studies in Political Thought* (London and New York, Routledge, 1993)

Eric Mack, 'Isaiah Berlin and the Quest for Liberal

Pluralism', *Public Affairs Quarterly* 7 No 3 (July 1993), 215–30

George Crowder, 'Pluralism and Liberalism', *Political Studies* 42 (1994), 293–305 (reply by Berlin and Bernard Williams, ibid., 306–9)

Arnaldo Momigliano, 'On the Pioneer Trail', review of *Vico and Herder* in *New York Review of Books*, 11 November 1976, 33–8

Patrick Gardiner, review of *Vico and Herder* in *History and Theory* 16 (1977), 45–51

Anyone interested in Berlin's attempt to marry value pluralism with liberalism should read Joseph Raz's books *The Morality of Freedom* (Oxford, Clarendon Press, 1986) and *Ethics in the Public Domain* (Oxford, Clarendon Press, 1994).

Issues of moral realism and relativism, closely relevant to Berlin's thought, are explored by Richard Rorty in his book *Contingency, Irony and Solidarity* (Cambridge, Cambridge University Press, 1989) and by Bernard Williams in his 'Replies' in J. E. J. Altham and Ross Harrison, eds., *World, Mind and Ethics: Essays on the Ethical Philosophy of Bernard Williams* (Cambridge, Cambridge University Press, 1995).

I am indebted to Henry Hardy for his invaluable assistance with this list of further reading.

JOHN GRAY
Jesus College, Oxford, April 1995

Index